## What Others Are Saying about
## David Skultety and *Ripple Marketing*

"David is someone whom anyone in the network marketing profession could learn from. His knowledge of what it takes to build a successful network marketing business is second to none. Whether you are brand new to network marketing, or already an established leader, the concepts and strategies inside of this book could be life-changing for your business. Anyone who has ever been fortunate enough to know or work with David understands exactly how special a leader he is, and his incredible ability to teach. Now everyone has access to his wisdom, knowledge, and experience by simply picking up and reading this book. I have no doubt that this book will become one of the 'must reads' for anyone inside of this great profession."

— Bob Heilig, President, Bob Heilig Media

"David is a true servant leader and his teaching and mentorship have been invaluable to me and my team. *Ripple Marketing* is a must have for all network marketing professionals looking to take their businesses and personal growth to the next level."

— Brandy Sinoto, Network Marketing Leader

I believe that *Ripple Marketing* may be the most comprehensive discussion to date of what it takes to win in network marketing. It is extremely well-written, thoughtful, and instructive on identifying the fundamentals necessary to succeed. It has just risen to the top of my recommended reading list for my team."

— John Terhune, Best-Selling Author, Internationally Acclaimed Keynote Speaker, and Attorney-at-Law

"*Ripple Marketing* is designed for those who want to take it to the next level. Dive in and discover why David Skultety has enjoyed remarkable success. His passion with purpose brings a rich perspective that will save you years in creating your success in network marketing."

— Dr. Taylor Hartman, Best-Selling Author
and Founder of the Color Code

"David Skultety encapsulates everything you need to know about the profession of network marketing with engaging stories, advice, and valuable training woven throughout this fun and easy read. His experience and insights gleaned over twenty years as a network marketing leader are invaluable. Whether you are a new distributor, a leader looking for the perfect 101 book for your team, or someone contemplating entering the profession, *Ripple Marketing* is the perfect go-to source."

— Sonia Magruder, Network Marketing Leader

"David Skultety has influenced thousands of people's lives in the two decades he's spent as a network marketing leader. In *Ripple Marketing*, he offers you insights and strategies on what it takes to build a successful long-term MLM business. Read and take action on what you're about to learn and you'll experience the game-changing value of this book."

— Simon Chan, Founder of MLM Nation

"I am proud to call David Skultety a friend and colleague. In his debut future best seller, you will get an inspiring first look at what you *can do* with this profession! A true 'how to' guide to success and building your business with passion and heart. David and Marcella are a wonderful example of how to do just that. In life and family, they are true examples of love and light. This is a *must read* if you want to be a network marketing professional."

— Dr. Dana McGrady, Network Marketing Leader


"Want to make it big in network marketing and completely transform your life and bank account? Start here!"

— Patrick Snow, Publishing Coaching and International Best-Selling Author of *Creating Your Own Destiny*


"Whether you are already with a company or in the beginning phases of exploring this lucrative profession, *Ripple Marketing* is the book to read! The book is easy and enjoyable to read while educating the beginner as well as the experienced networker who wants to build it huge with competence, excellence, and ease!"

— Renate Lundberg, Network Marketing Leader


"*Ripple Marketing* is a must-read for all network marketing professionals. It's easy to read and to the point, but more importantly, it's proven, step-by-step strategies for success in network marketing are easy to follow. I recommend this book to everyone in our profession. It's full of brilliant stories and examples from David's real-world, hands-on experiences, like how to launch a new person's business for maximum momentum. Whether you're brand new or a veteran of this profession, you will find invaluable insights and lessons."

— Garrett McGrath, President, Association of Network Marketing Professionals

"David's book takes you on a personal journey from first look to advancing his way through a lifelong and highly successful career in network marketing. Anyone wanting to make it big in network marketing should devour this book and use what's being taught here!"

— Todd Falcone, Network Marketing Speaker, Coach, and Author

# RIPPLE
## MARKETING

FROM RIPPLE TO WAVE—BUILDING
IT HUGE IN NETWORK MARKETING

# DAVID SKULTETY

Steve,
Great connecting andtalking
w/ you. Keep on rocking
life. Hope to cross paths soon.

**AVIVA**
PUBLISHING
New York

RIPPLE MARKETING
From Ripple to Wave—Building It HUGE in Network Marketing

Published by Ripple Marketing, LLC

www.DavidSkultety.com

ISBN: 9781944335540
Library of Congress: 2017900831

Editor: Tyler Tichelaar/Superior Book Productions
Cover Design: Nicole Gabriel/Angel Dog Productions
Interior Book Layout: Nicole Gabriel/Angel Dog Productions
Author Photo: Geralyn Camarillo & Arna Johnson

Every attempt has been made to source properly all quotes

Printed in the United States of America

First Edition

**2 4 6 8 10 12**

# DEDICATION

To my wife, Marcella:

You are my best friend, lover, and an amazing mother to our three children. Thank you for believing in me when I didn't believe in myself. You have supported me with all of my entrepreneurial endeavors and been my biggest advocate. I love you deeply with all my heart and soul.

To my children, Drew, Grace, and Catherine:

I am so proud to be your father. Each of you is unique in your own way and your futures are bright. As I've always told you, follow your passion and you will never work a day in your life.

To my parents, Ernie and Eileen:

Words cannot express how much I love you. I appreciate the life lessons you have taught me over the years. Mom, your nurturing and sacrifices put me in the position to grow into the man I am today. Dad, your risk-taking as an entrepreneur taught me the value of controlling my own destiny. I am forever grateful for the unwavering support you both have offered over the last fifty years.

To my network marketing friends and colleagues:

You can't get to the top without helping others advance. I am forever grateful to the leaders I have worked with and learned from over the past two-plus decades. Every concept or principle in this book came from someone I consider a mentor. So many friends gained. So many roads traveled.

# ACKNOWLEDGMENTS

Over the past two decades that I have been building my business, I've been supported by a lot of people who have offered their time to mentor, guide, and inspire me on my journey to becoming a network marketing professional.

I would like to thank my friend David Litt for his leadership and guidance. David is one of the hardest-working corporate executives in network marketing. If it wasn't for him, I would not have been put in the situation to write this book. I'm truly grateful for his wisdom and integrity in always doing the right thing. His encouragement to put my experience on paper will provide a ripple effect to future entrepreneurs looking to succeed in this profession.

Throughout my career, I've been inspired by many leaders within the network marketing profession, but one stands out among the crowd: Brandy Sinoto. She and I have enjoyed a seventeen-year friendship and business partnership. Her critical thinking, leadership, and work ethic motivated me to write this book, and I will be forever grateful and proud for what we have accomplished together. The best is yet to come.

I would like to thank Patrick Snow for giving me guidance and the encouragement that I could write a book on my own. I would also like to thank my editor, Tyler Tichelaar, and my layout and cover designer, Nicole Gabriel.

# CONTENTS

# FOREWORD

I really enjoy playing poker. Texas Hold 'em in particular. And there is a saying about this game that rings true for network marketing as well—"It takes a minute to learn…and a lifetime to master."

Think about it for a second.

Network marketing is so simple. You try a product or service. You are pleased with the results. You share that product or service with some of your favorite people. They try it. The company that manufactures the product or provides the service then pays you a small referral fee as a "thank you." And if any of the people whom you refer, in turn refer people, you also get referral fees for their purchases. And if these people refer people, you get more referral fees. And so on. That's really it.

Use. Share. Earn. Repeat.

Use. Share. Earn. Repeat.

There. One minute and you understand the network marketing business model.

Or is it really that simple?

Which product or service should you represent? How do you

launch your business? Whom do you contact? Which tools should you use? What about social media and technology? And events? How do you share your success story? And how do you systematize your business so you can teach others to do what you did? What happens when your network grows? What happens when your network stops growing? What do you do when you face adversity?

Suddenly, the program that takes a minute to learn gets a bit more complicated. And if you want to "master" it…if you want to build a big team, capitalize on this powerful business model and earn life-changing income…then you need a guide to lead you on this fun, exciting, and sometimes confusing journey.

That's why I'm so glad you are reading this book.

Just like you wouldn't go surfing on the North Shore of Hawaii by yourself, you shouldn't try to become a network marketing professional without learning from an industry leader who has "conquered the biggest waves in the world" more than once.

David Skultety is your Big Wave Surfing Guide. David has grown two different network marketing teams from 1 to 100,000 people. And I was along for the ride on both of these exciting (and lucrative) journeys. He knows the attitude and energy you must possess to jump on the board in the first place. Then he will lead you beyond the surf zone, get you paddling fast, and up on your feet. He will talk you through the wipeouts until you are carving like a local. And if you stay true to the lessons, soon enough you could be tacking a twenty-footer off of Pipeline!

And, most importantly, once you've got things figured out for yourself, David will inspire you to help others follow in your wake.

Is it worth it?

There are people in my life who have lots of money and very little time. There are people in my life who have lots of time and very little money. But the only people in my life who have lots of money and lots of time are my friends who are network marketing professionals like David. People who have taken this amazing journey, riding the big waves. People who understand the difference between owning a business and owning their lives.

Are you ready?

Let me offer one last quick story to inspire you even more.

At the time, I was a senior-level marketing executive in the network marketing industry for more than a dozen years. And I kept seeing this quote from J. Paul Getty which says, "I would rather be paid on 1 percent of the efforts of 100 people, than 100 percent of my own efforts." This quote was used to explain the concept of leverage and the financial potential of building a business based on a large network of people.

And the more I read this quote, the more I was convinced it was wrong.

I just didn't get it.

It seemed like simple math to me. If I profit from 1 percent of the efforts of 100 average people, then I am receiving the value of 100 average units. But I consider myself above average. So my own efforts would net a value of 100 above-average units. 100 above-average units are more valuable than 100 average units. The numbers didn't add up. So I was certain I was smarter than this old billionaire.

Well, not surprisingly, I was wrong. I am not smarter than a billionaire.

The fault in my logic is simple. If I utilized the 1 percent of 100 other people's efforts, I would still have 100 percent of my own efforts to put to good use on other projects. On the other hand, if I utilized 100 percent of my own efforts (even if they did produce above average results), I would have 0 percent left for anything else.

So, if you are like I was, an above-average person who feels like you have 0 percent left for anything else, read this book on how to build a network. David Skultety is about to teach you how to build a residual income based on the efforts of other people. Sure, it is going to take your own efforts to get the first level of your network in place, but ultimately this book is a blueprint for long-term financial freedom. Financial freedom...that is the goal.

You've got no time to waste.

The ripple is turning into a wave.

Your guide is waiting.

Get ready to drop in.

There's a big one headed your way.

Surf's up!

David Litt

Network Marketing Corporate Executive

# THE LIBERATING PROFESSION

If you've picked up this book, you're likely on a quest to make your business and your life better. Maybe you're sick of feeling like you're stuck in a rut. Maybe you're looking for a new career. Maybe you have tried many different ways to earn a living but none of them has worked out for you.

I have great news for you! You are someone who doesn't settle. You want more in life. You have a hunger inside of you—a hunger for success—and that is the first thing you need to succeed. Now I'm going to share with you the tools you need to make that dream of success your reality—through network marketing.

In these pages, I am going to share with you the key success principles that will help you succeed in your network marketing business: mindset, action, team, and leadership. The book is divided into four sections, one for each of these principles.

I am going to teach you how to develop the proper success mindset. Together, we will explore what you have to do to build that mindset quickly and what factors will be necessary for you to sustain it for the long haul. I'll highlight several invaluable lessons that I learned that will help you not only become a leader, but attract the right people to your organization. I'll teach you what you have to do and how to do it. I'll even touch base on the power of dreams and how to create that unshakable belief that can propel you to network marketing stardom.

If you internalize and apply these principles and concepts, you will shave years off your learning curve and become a more productive network marketer. You'll become a leader whom people will follow, and you will position yourself to empower others to greatness.

You may be chasing your dreams and want network marketing to be the vehicle to achieve them. You may be part-time but have aspirations of becoming a full-time network marketing professional. You may have had some success, or you may feel like you have failed and are not suited for this business. I just want you to know that I have walked in your shoes, and wherever you currently are, it's okay. Accept where you are and realize that I believe in you and want to help you believe in yourself.

I recognize that there a lot of resources and coaches available to guide you toward the success you are looking for, so I'm grateful that you have considered me to help you. I want to serve as your coach, mentor, and partner for success. Along your journey, I hope to be a resource you can look toward. My primary goal is to help you succeed and attract as many people as possible to this liberating profession.

As you read through this book, I encourage you to highlight sections that offer you any aha moments. Each chapter has an exercise at the end to help you expand on a principle or concept. Be sure to spend the time to complete them since they will help you to internalize the concepts until you think and act like a true network marketer.

So are you ready to learn what it takes to succeed in network marketing? Are you longing to become a true network marketing profession-al? If so, let's get started. Your time is now!

I wish you much success on this journey—may your network always ripple!

David Skultety

# My Path to Becoming a Network Marketing Professional

*"I alone can't change the world, but I can cast a stone across the waters to create many ripples."*

— Mother Teresa

I grew up in a Pittsburgh suburb in a middle class family. My dad was a pharmacist and my mom stayed home to take care of my brother, sister, and me as we grew up. It seemed as though my parents made just enough money to provide for us year in and year out. They sent us to good schools, put us through college, and achieved their goals of giving us more than their parents were able to give them. My parents are awesome, and I am forever grateful to them for everything they have provided my siblings and me with over the years.

In 1979, when I was twelve, my dad was transferred to New Jersey with the company he worked for. It was a very impressionable time for me when I was very open to exploration. The friends I made at the time were all riding mopeds to get around, so I wanted one. I asked my mom and dad whether I could have one. Their response was a turning point in my life. They told me that I could have anything I wanted in life, but I would have to work for it. After discussing it, and getting an understanding of what they were saying, it became clear that I needed to do something if I were going to make some money to buy one myself. What to do?

For those of you too young to remember, in the late '70s, there was an oil embargo so gasoline had to be rationed. As a result, if you wanted to get gas for your car, you needed to wait in long lines, every other day, based on your license plate number. In the town where I lived, it was not uncommon to see over 100 cars lined up along the road to get access to the gas station.

My friend Kevin and I had the idea of setting up a coffee stand on the roadside to sell coffee and lemonade to the frustrated individuals waiting their turns to get gas. This early business venture worked out pretty well because our cost of goods sold was zero since Kevin's dad worked in the supermarket business and for some reason had a bunch of excess coffee and lemonade mix in his garage. Talk about *free* enterprise.

Needless to say, we had a captive audience, a no-cost inventory, and a line of people who needed their caffeine and sugar high to get them by while they waited in line. It was my first entrepreneurial endeavor, and I saved several hundred dollars. Not enough for the new Safari moped I had my eyes on, but I had created my first entrepreneurial ripple.

When summer ended, I entered middle school. The first week of school while riding the bus, I noticed a girl who always had a pack of gum; everyone would ask her for a piece until she didn't have any more left. This sparked the idea of my selling gum to everyone. It ended up being a brilliant idea. I started with just enough inventory to take care of the kids on the bus, but it quickly escalated to purchasing enough gum to sell to everyone in the sixth grade. Demand was high and profits were even higher. I branched out to carry a line of Jolly Ranchers, and they, too, were a huge hit. The run lasted for several months, until a couple of kids saw my wad of dollar bills and what seemed to be five pounds of coins I stuffed into my pockets before homeroom every day. Copycats started to emerge; the extra supply drove the price down, and along with it, the profits. That didn't matter. I was making a solid twenty dollars per day, as a sixth grader, back in 1979. That was pretty good coin back then, considering that minimum wage was $2.90. Needless to say, I saved enough money to buy my moped. Life was good!

This experience, or "life lesson," that my parents taught me really opened my thoughts to what could be. I really became motivated by finding ways to make money. When the winter season rolled in and the snow fell, I would shovel driveways. When the spring thaw arrived and the grass started growing, I would cut lawns. I even got paid for watering lawns when there was a water shortage. While in high school, I started an auto detailing business that lasted until I went to college. Because of all of this entrepreneurial activity, I made enough money to purchase mopeds, motorcycles, and, ultimately, my first car, a 1976 Datsun 280 Z.

I was very blessed to have parents who were committed to putting their children through college. I was told that I should go to college, get a degree, and go get a job. I went to Drexel University in Philadelphia, but I had no idea what I wanted to do.

My college experience was really good. Yes, I learned a lot, but the real fun lay in all the free-thinking exploration I was introduced to. There were two core parts of my college experience that shaped me into becoming the lifestyle entrepreneur I am today: the internship program at Drexel and the Grateful Dead.

While I was still a high school freshman, a friend had taken me to see the Grateful Dead in concert. At the time, I had no idea who the Grateful Dead was, but the experience was, let's just say, unique. Once I got to college, I pledged a fraternity where a handful of the brothers were Deadheads. And that's when I got on "The Bus."

I really enjoyed the Grateful Dead's music and the experience I had going to their concerts. Each show I attended was a time to let go of all my stress and worries, expand my mind, and get a sense of what path I wanted to take in life.

I learned a lot about entrepreneurship from the Grateful Dead. For one, their tours were like a traveling circus. They had a huge following; Deadheads would travel from city to city to hear the music and experience the experience. Most people who followed the band had very little money, so they would sell everything from tie-dyes to grilled cheese sandwiches to earn enough for a ticket, let alone gas to get to the next city. I really respected the Deadheads for their dedication to their passion. Yes, a handful of them were lost in space, but they were some of the most resilient individuals I've ever associated with. They taught me the importance of being able to face adversity, having a "Never quit" attitude, and being grateful for what you have.

And then there was the music. The music of the Grateful Dead was unique, and it clearly was an acquired taste. In many respects, it wasn't the songs they played as much as how they played them. Those who know the music understand that the band wasn't the best at what it did; it was the only band that did what it did. It mastered the art of improvising. Every show was different because each night when the band members walked on stage, they didn't have a set list. They would start playing, and depending on the mood and circumstances, individual band members would lead everyone else into the next song. It was this improvising that taught me the importance of being flexible in business, and in life. Sometimes, you just have to let nature take its course. I also learned about the importance of working as a team and of allowing those who are leading, the opportunity to lead. I learned many life and entrepreneurial lessons on the road with the Grateful Dead over the years, and I don't think I would be who I am today without them.

The second major influence on my entrepreneurial career was Drexel's internship program. It had a cooperative education program in which you went to school for six months and then worked in the industry of your choice for the next six. My first co-op was with Mobile Oil in its marketing and credit card processing department. I learned one thing from that experience: Corporate America was not for me.

My second co-op employer was National Theme Productions, a costume company that put Halloween kiosks in J.C. Penney's and Sears stores across the country. The job was actually really cool. I was a regional sales manager for the North Jersey/New York markets. I learned a lot about marketing and dealing with people. And I also learned that I didn't want to be responsible for a lot of employees.

In my last two years of college, I became interested in finance and did my third co-op in London, England, for the investment banking and retail brokerage firm, Shearson Lehman Hutton. Based on that experience, I decided I wanted a career on Wall Street—everything was moving in that direction. Unfortunately, I graduated in the spring of 1990, a year that brought a pretty significant economic recession, so Wall Street was not hiring. To this day, I still have the seventy-plus rejection letters from every investment bank I applied to.

College degree, but no job! So where does one go? Europe seemed to be the logical answer. My friend Charlie and I embarked on a three-month bicycle ride across Western Europe. But to make it worthy of a resume, we decided to do it for a cause and call it a fundraiser. So we looked in the phone book, talked to a couple of people, and decided the Multiple Sclerosis Association of America was a great organization to represent. We crafted a press release, talked Giant Bicycle into donating us some wheels, purchased a plane ticket, and away we went. In all, ten weeks of riding, three thousand miles, many great experiences, and a lot of soul searching about what I would do with my life when I got back.

Upon returning home, the economy was still a little soft, so I resorted to what I knew: entrepreneurism. I started a business down at the Jersey Shore with my friend Frank. It was an advertising business in which we placed business card displays in high traffic areas such as restaurants, grocery stores, and car washes. We expanded to offer a coupon magazine and aerial advertising along the beach. It was a lot of fun. I learned a lot, but because it was a seasonal business, we really didn't make enough money for both of us to make a living.

In 1994, the economy was getting strong, so I decided to apply for the Wall Street job I ultimately wanted. I landed a job in the private client division of Kidder Peabody. On my first day in the office, the infamous Joseph Jett bond scandal was front page and center on *The Wall Street Journal*. Within twenty-four hours, Kidder canceled the training class I was supposed to enter and my branch manager suggested there wasn't a job. Ultimately, General Electric sold Kidder to PaineWebber, so I entered the next training class.

It was only a couple of months after I completed my training when I received "the call." You know, the call from a friend who wants you to look at some business opportunity. In my case, it was a guy named Kelly who played golf with my dad. He asked whether I would be interested in making money on the deregulation of the telecom industry. My interest was piqued. He took me to a local office complex where I was first introduced to "drawing circles." I was amazed at the simplicity of the presentation and how it all made sense. All I heard in the presentation were three words: passive residual income. What a concept. At that meeting, the presenter suggested that everyone attend a regional event the following weekend in Baltimore.

It was at that event that I saw the big picture. Seven thousand people attended, and I was captivated by all the stories told from the stage. People from all kinds of backgrounds were succeeding with this company. One story really caught my attention: the story of a guy I knew from college. We had not been friends, but I would see him on campus at a particular fraternity house from time to time. Let's just say he wasn't the model student. As a matter of fact, I think he majored in partying. To my surprise, he was recognized for achieving the company's top rank and making over $20,000 per month. Well, you know what I said to myself, *If he can do it, so can I.*

I spent the next couple of years trying to build a business on a part-time basis. I really wanted it to work, but as I look back on the experience, I was destined to fail. I wasn't coachable, didn't follow the system, was afraid to talk to the right people, rarely did three-way calls, and made myself the issue every step of the way. As a matter of fact, I didn't do anything right. After three years, the residual income check I was dreaming about was less than $100 per month. I considered myself a failure.

At that time, one of the leaders I was under decided to leave the company for a start-up company. I followed. That was a mistake! I left a good company for a start-up based in Sarasota, Florida. It was only a couple of months until I realized that the owner of that company wasn't operating with the highest integrity so I quit. All I could think about at that point was the mistake I had made taking time away from building my asset management business to chase a dream with network marketing. It wasn't for me.

Fast forward two years to March 1999. A guy named Harris, whom I had met during my short experience with that last company, called me to ask whether I would be interested in evaluating a new company. I was not interested, but I listened to what he had to say. Then I was a little intrigued for a couple of reasons: the company was going to distribute nutritional products and was being led by a former president and CEO of one of the largest and oldest direct sales companies. Long story short, I joined that company as a founding associate and ending up building a business that enrolled over 300,000 customers and produced over $500 million in wholesale sales.

I spent over a decade building that business and learning a lot about network marketing. The experience was a complete turnaround compared to my first network marketing endeavor. I made a lot of good friends and learned what to do, and more importantly, what not to do when building a business. A great income was earned, but it was the intangible benefits that changed my life: the ability to work from home, be present for our children, coach baseball, take vacations when I wanted to, and make friends that would last a lifetime.

Between 2009 and 2013, I took a break from building my business. I spent my time with my family, enjoyed the fruits of my labor, and even took on a couple of consulting jobs helping companies with their marketing strategy and systems. In the summer of 2013, I was approached by a friend who is an industry executive to assist him in crafting a marketing plan for a company that was looking to grow. After several months of work, I realized that there was an opportunity to get back in the field and build it again from scratch. It was a scary proposition since I knew how hard it could be, but a decision was made to build it big again and that's what we did. Just like we did with the previous endeavor, we went to work and built an organization from 1-100,000 people. Although this time much faster.

Looking back, each team we built started with a ripple. That first exposure led to that first enrollment. We created one ripple after another until they swelled into waves of activity that led to amazing income and newfound lifestyles for many on our team.

It wasn't always a smooth road, but the lessons I learned were priceless. So much so that I felt compelled to write this book and share what I learned along my journey. I hope sharing my experiences will benefit you like they have me. If they do, then my journey will have been all worthwhile.

# WHY NETWORK MARKETING?

"Network marketing is the big wave of the future. It's taking the place of franchising which now requires too much capital for the average person."

— Jim Rohn

My father was a pharmacist by trade. He started his career working for the largest drugstore chain in the country, and over a twenty-two-year period, he made his way up the ranks to a district manager position. Like many people in corporate America, he hit a glass ceiling; when he was turned down for a promotion he deserved, he decided to leave the company and start his own pharmacy business.

I'm sure this move was exciting and terrifying for him at the same time. He had lost his predictable income, but he was taking control of his own destiny. He had to get a loan to start the business, invest in inventory, hire employees, rent commercial space, provide employee benefits, and pay for all the other incidental overhead it takes to run a small business. All of this before he sold his first prescription, let alone pay himself any salary.

It was a big risk, and my father made several huge sacrifices in the process. He commuted from New Jersey to Pittsburgh, and we only saw him every other weekend. It was not easy on my mom, who had the challenge of raising three young children. Times were thin, but my parents persevered. At the time, I probably took my parents' sacrifices and risk-taking for granted, but now as I look back, I'm so proud of what they accomplished, and I'm grateful for the lessons and work ethic they taught me.

However, the weight of the overhead and other factors ultimately pushed my dad's business into bankruptcy. Looking back, that was a turning point for my parents. They were at a fork in the road— my dad could go out and find a job, or borrow more money and start over again. I really appreciate the decision my dad made. He had a dream, and he was committed to doing whatever necessary to support his family without reentering the corporate world. So he reached out to a family member, borrowed more money, and bought an existing pharmacy in New Jersey. It was great to have him back in the home, but most of the time, he was only there to sleep because he worked seventy- to eighty-hour work weeks, sometimes more. Eventually, through commitment and perseverance, he succeeded as an entrepreneur and provided for his family in amazing ways. Today, he is now living the retirement lifestyle of his dreams.

These days, not too many people can do what my father did. People don't have the capital, banks have tough lending policies, and competition from the Internet has changed the landscape of many industries. To start a traditional small business today, one has to incur many risks.

The annual saving rate in America today is at an all-time low. Most people have not saved enough for retirement. The average consumer credit card debt is at an all-time high of about $16,000 per household. People are living beyond their means and trying to live lifestyles they can't afford. All of this within an economy that is being artificially propped up by zero interest rates and consumers increasing their levels of personal debt.

Income levels for the average American between 2003 and 2015 increased 26 percent. But the cost of living has outpaced this figure significantly. Health care costs over the same period are up 51 percent and going higher, and food and beverage costs are up over 37 percent. All indications suggest these trends will continue.

On top of all this, there is no job security today. More and more jobs are being outsourced or placed in the hands of younger millennials who are willing to do the work at a lower salary, sent to people outside the United States, or even given to robots. People are working longer hours and making less. There are more single parents today than any other time in U.S. history, and family lifestyles are being compromised by the need to work multiple jobs just to make ends meet. The combination of all these factors brings human stress levels to an unhealthy state.

Can you relate? Take a moment and think about it. Who do you know who has any of the issues I'm referring to? What are people going to do to remedy the situations they are in? I'm watching people everywhere I go ignore the reality of their financial landscape while they simply hope for a brighter future. They have stopped dreaming of what can be and have become very complacent. The entitlement mindset is spreading through our society while few take a proactive stance against the inevitable challenges.

On the other hand, an entrepreneurial movement is happening in which people are taking ownership of their futures and controlling their own destinies. Some of these individuals are sick and tired of being sick and tired with living the status quo. Others have just realized that they didn't plan well, so they have no other choice but to build a business of their own.

The millennials have just surpassed the baby boomers in size. They see what their parents have gone through and don't want anything to do with it. They think differently, want more, and are going to get it on their own terms.

And then there are what I call the "successful discontents." These people have been successful in their careers or other business ventures and are looking to build lifestyle businesses on their own terms by leveraging their experiences and relationships. They want businesses that have no overhead, no employees, no inventory, no commute, and unlimited income potential. Where are they all flocking to? The profession of network marketing.

When people ask me what I do for a living, I usually turn it around by asking them a question: "What do you know about network marketing?" Every time I ask that question, I get a different answer. What's amazing to me is how many people do not know what network marketing is, how it works, or the amazing lifestyle it can provide.

Network marketing, for those of you who are new to the concept, is a business model that a company uses to distribute its products or services. It is driven by independent distributors who market the products or services to end users, usually people they know, like friends and family. In exchange, the company they represent will pay them a referral commission for the initial sale, plus an ongoing royalty for as long as that customer uses the product or service.

The business model becomes really powerful when one elects to build an organization of distributors. If done right, you can leverage your efforts so they multiply by the thousands. This leverage can put you in a situation to build residual income that can totally change your financial wellbeing, not to mention the peace of mind necessary to live a grateful life.

When compared to a traditional business, the benefits of the network marketing model are significant. In a traditional brick-and-mortar business, you are faced with a large capital investment, employees, insurance, a commercial lease, and other expenses.

Thousands of Americans make this brick-and-mortar commitment every year, but the success rate of new traditional business is very low. According to Bloomberg, eight out of ten entrepreneurs who start businesses fail within the first eighteen months. A whopping 80 percent crash and burn! That's a lot of risk and time spent chasing the American Dream with nothing to show for it. Not that you don't learn something from such endeavors, but I know that for the average person, there is a better way. A way that is less risky, more fun, less stressful, and potentially a lot more profitable.

So, why network marketing? The benefits of network marketing are vast, especially when compared to traditional business. Following are just a few of the key benefits and reasons why network marketing is such a viable solution for entrepreneurs today.

**Low Investment**
When one joins a network marketing company, the typical investment is $500 or less. Obviously, with such a low investment, there is a low barrier to entry and very little risk. Interestingly enough, that benefit can pose a challenge for some because without a large investment, it makes it easy to quit and not take a financial hit. But let's focus on the positive. Anyone can afford to start a network marketing business.

**Home-Based Entrepreneurship**
Because your business will be home-based, it will reduce your overhead and risk considerably. Another great advantage is you will have a really short commute. For me, it has been about thirty feet down the hall. I love having the ability to work from home. I was able to see our children off to school, be there when they returned home, and be available pretty much on demand. Being home is one of the primary benefits of having a network marketing business.

**Tax Advantages**
I'm not a CPA, but in my opinion, every person in America should have a home-based business. The IRS states that as long as you are in the pursuit of profit, you have the ability to deduct certain business expenses associated with operating your business. Things like your cell phone, Internet access, car payments, home office deductions, travel and entertainment, health insurance premiums, and marketing are all expenses that may be tax deductible. The average person could save several thousand dollars in taxes each year just by being self-employed within the network marketing profession. Remember, it's not what you make; it's what you keep.

**No Borders**
Another great benefit to network marketing is that there are no borders to where you can potentially market your product. Network marketing is a $183 billion global business. If your company is operating just in United States, you can build a business in any state. And if your company operates internationally, you are only limited to the countries in which it is registered and has operations. With the companies I have represented, I have been able to get paid on product sales in the United States, Canada, Europe, and Asia. I have friends within the profession who literally get paid 24/7 on global networks they have built. Companies that expand internationally create seamless compensation plans, translate mar-

keting materials, provide satellite offices with support, and much more. Where else can you build an international business from the comfort of your own home?

## Part-Time

More than 80 percent of the 103 million people who represent a network marketing company do so on a part-time basis. They do it to supplement their incomes and potentially make it a full-time endeavor. Over the years, I've helped thousands of people start a part-time network marketing business. Many of them were able to earn an extra $500 per month to pay for a car payment, a couple of thousand per month to pay for the rent or mortgage, and even earn six-figures on a part-time basis. The main point is: Network marketing offers the average person the ability to build a business on a part-time basis that could help eliminate credit card debt, pay for an education, provide retirement income, or even fund a long overdue family vacation. Just think about what it would mean to have an extra $500, $1,000, or even $10,000 per month in extra income. What would you do with it?

You don't have to quit your job, move to a new city, or mortgage your house to start a network marketing business. You just need to make a decision, carve out the time you are willing to commit to your future, and get to work.

## Flexibility and Time Freedom

One of the core reasons people are flocking to network marketing is to gain more flexibility and time freedom in their lives. As an employee, you are told when to show up, what to do, and when you can take time for yourself and your family. As a traditional business owner, you could find yourself being owned by your business.

Earlier, I illustrated my father's business story. For years, he owned a business that owned him. That didn't last forever, but he didn't have the time, freedom, and flexibility he wanted when he was building his business. What I've enjoyed with building my network marketing business is the flexibility to take time off when needed, spend time with family and friends, and work where I want, when I want. As a matter of fact, as I write this, it's a Tuesday morning and I am flying down to Augusta, Georgia to attend the Masters Tournament. That time freedom and flexibility would probably not be available if I were someone else's employee. I'm truly grateful for this profession.

## Leverage

As an employee or owner of a small business, you can only work so many hours. The average full-time employee works forty hours per week. The average self-employed small business owner works sixty hours per week. In both roles, you may be caught up in multiple duties and wearing multiple hats. In network marketing, you get to leverage other people's time, resources, efforts, brain power, and money. You can build a sales organization of part-time and full-time distributors who are each going to work toward their personal business' success.

Imagine if you built a team of fifty people, and each of them put five hours per week into his or her business. That's a total of 250 collective hours spent toward the growth of your business. That's leverage! Over the years, I've been able to leverage thousands of part-time people, each working a couple of hours per week. In addition, I've been able to partner with people of influence, people with marketing skills, talented speakers and trainers, and a host of other people who possessed talents I didn't have. All of these people had more to offer than I did, and I was able not only to learn from their experiences, but to get paid for their efforts and skills. What a concept!

## Social Media Leverage

The future of marketing in general is going to be driven through content delivery via social media, and network marketing is poised to benefit in this area more than any other industry. With Facebook, Instagram, Snap Chat, and other social media platforms, the world is getting smaller. We are now in a position to literally have six degrees of separation from anyone in the world. Those who learn the art of leveraging social media position themselves not only to build a successful business, but to do so faster and more efficiently than ever before.

**Lifestyle and Exotic Trips**
One of the great aspects of network marketing that we have enjoyed over the years is the lifestyle it can afford. I'm not talking about the lifestyles of the rich and famous, but the way people live when they become successful in network marketing. Not having to answer to anyone but yourself can be very rewarding. And if you make it to a leadership position within your company's plan, you will experience amazing recognition trips that you would never get in the general workforce. Over the last twenty years we have been flown all around the world to places like Hawaii, Mexico, China, and other exotic destinations to experience lifestyle resorts and everything that comes with them.

**Income Potential**
Speaking of getting paid, the final benefit I would like to highlight is the income potential—not so much the amount of income, but the type of income. Network marketing companies offer you the opportunity to earn a referral commission every time you refer someone to the company who purchases its products or services. But the real power of most compensation plans is the ability to earn a residual income. Residual income is income you earn on the recurring orders of customers within your organization.

Responsible leaders in the network marketing profession do not make income claims, so all I'm going to say here is that there are no limits to what you can earn. A lot of people who represent network marketing companies on a part-time basis earn enough to pay for their products plus an extra $500 per month. Many others make thousands per month, tens of thousands per month, and I even know dozens of leaders within our profession who make a million dollars per year or more.

Network marketing is not the only way. I just see it as a better way for the average person to get ahead through entrepreneurship. It's not for everyone, but if you're reading this book, chances are you are looking to succeed with this business model. The chapters that follow will offer many of the key principles you will need to understand to ensure that success.

# Part I

# Starting With You

"Whether you think you can, or think you can't, you're right."

— Henry Ford

Life in general is directed and steered by a web of decisions and actions taken over time. Entrepreneurship—or more specifically, building a network marketing business—is no different.

To succeed in business, you need to possess or learn many skill sets. Before you can take the action necessary to build a business, some decisions need to be made and mental thoughts adjusted. They include having a dream, cultivating the proper mindset, building belief, knowing why you want to build a business, and being able to decide to take action.

As with any adjustment, it starts with putting the first foot forward. That first step you make will create a ripple that can lead to a whole new you. This first section will focus on getting your mental game plan in order.

## CHAPTER 1

# DREAMING BIG

"All our dreams can come true, if we have the
courage to pursue them."

— Walt Disney

What is your dream? Think about that for a minute. Do you even have one? If you could paint the canvas of your future life, what would it look like?

The power of a dream or vision for your future is one of the essential keys to succeeding with your network marketing business. If you wake up with a burning desire in your heart to accomplish your dreams, you will blow past the people who wake up seeking only next week's paycheck.

I'm so very grateful to have witnessed so many people achieve their dreams through this awesome profession. One example is my friend whose name is MaryKay. When she entered our business, I asked her what dreams she had, and how she wanted her network marketing business to play a role in those dreams. Several years earlier, she, like many others, was affected by the 2008 financial crisis. She had accumulated an overwhelming amount of consumer debt and was forced to leave the home she owned.

All she could think about was her dream of building a new home, but not just any home—she wanted to build her dream home. We talked about the sacrifices it would take, the long hours she would have to work at her business, and the course of action that would be necessary to achieve her goals. Nothing was going to stand in her way of achieving that dream. She visualized it, talked about it with her family and friends, and shared it with her business partners. Every morning, she awoke with a burning desire to take action so she could move one step closer to her dream.

I'm grateful to be able to say that not only did she achieve her dream of building her dream home, but she was able to make enough money to do so within two years of starting her network marketing business. In the process, she also was able to pay off all of her consumer debt. Today, she is living the dream in her new home without the stress of credit card debt, which handcuffs so many people financially across the country.

As with everything in life, it all starts with you. If you can get to the point where your daily method of operation is emotionally attached to achieving your dream, you will move mountains in this profession. If you can learn to help others do the same, you will develop passionate and productive leaders who will take you to the top of those mountains.

The first step in achieving your dream is to have one. You may need to dive into your inner self to get a real feel and understanding for what you want in life. Ask yourself questions like:

- What makes me happy?
- What am I most passionate about?

- What are my core values?
- What do I want for myself and my family?
- Where and how do I want to live?
- What does it look like?
- How do I feel when I visualize these thoughts?

Once you define your dream, you need to own it. It's one thing to have it in your head; it's another to have it on paper so you can visualize it every day. One way is to create a dream board.

My family has made it a custom to create individual dream boards every year around the New Year. We gather a bunch of magazines that highlight the topics we are passionate about. We page through them and cut out pictures, images, and words that relate to some of our New Year's goals and long-term dreams. Then we paste them on construction paper to create a collage that really shows our individual personalities and what we are passionate about. Finally, to cement the process, we take turns presenting our dream boards to each other. The boards are kept in a place where we can see them every day so we can be reminded of our dreams. It's really cool to do this process with my kids because it teaches them the importance and power of having dreams.

However, having dreams and accomplishing them are two different things. I've come across many people during my journey who talk about their goals and dreams, but they never achieve them. They feel that network marketing can be that vehicle to help them accomplish their goals, but for a handful of reasons, or excuses, it doesn't happen.

I believe the reason why these people remain stagnant is because their dreams are not big enough and they have not figured out how to make them heart-centered. When your dreams become personal and heart-centered, you will have more drive to take the actions necessary to make them come true. When you inject some passion into your dreams, you gather more energy around them and your motivation to achieve them is increased. Passion and motivation are critical if you want to achieve your dreams and aspirations.

To help you accomplish your dreams with your network marketing business, I have seven simple but powerful pieces of advice:

1.  **It's Going to Take Some Time:** "Rome wasn't built in a day." It's going to take some time to build a business that will help you achieve your dreams. Today, we live in an instant gratification society where people want things on demand. Well, success in your network marketing business is not going to happen overnight. Some businesses grow faster than others, but having the patience to run the marathon of business building is important to acknowledge and accept.

2.  **Find a Mentor:** If you have a particular dream you want to achieve and you see someone within your company who is living that dream, follow that person. If you can't find a mentor in your company, look elsewhere. Your mentor should have the same values as you and be willing to share his or her experiences that will guide you in the right direction.

3.  **Take Consistent Action:** Action is where the rubber meets the road. Action speaks louder than words. If you want to achieve your dreams, you need to do what most people are afraid to do once they wake up from their state of dreaming. Know what you should be doing day in and day out to move your business forward. Stop studying the compensation plan, learning about your products, and organizing your office space. Get engaged in the *income-producing activities* you need to be doing to make the money necessary to achieve your dreams. And be consistent. It's that simple!

4. **Learn from Your Mistakes:** We all make mistakes. You can either get knocked down from them or grow from them. It's your choice. When you make a mistake, acknowledge it, learn from it, and grow from it. Chances are you will not make that mistake again, and you will be able to keep others from making it themselves. I've made plenty of mistakes and errors in judgment over the years while building my business, but I credit these mistakes with a lot of the success I've had. Don't allow a mistake or setback to keep you from achieving your dreams. The path to achieving your dreams is not necessarily going to be a smooth ride. Stay on the journey and make course corrections along the way.

5. **Be Inspired by Others:** Everyone needs inspiration in his or her life, and network marketing offers plenty of it. While in pursuit of your dreams, be inspired by what is possible and by others who have accomplished what you seek. While in pursuit of network marketing success, look up to those field leaders in your company who have blazed the path before you. If you can't find inspirational leaders in your company, attend one of the annual industry events and get inspired by leaders in other companies. Look outside the box. There are plenty of inspiring entrepreneurs doing great things in traditional business. There are plenty of inspiring public and church leaders doing great things as well. Bottom line, look for inspiration in everything you do and it will help you with the process of achieving your dreams.

6. **Celebrate Along the Way:** Achieving your dreams is a journey. Along that journey, you will have little wins. Celebrate them and the wins of others on your team. Be grateful for where you are and the path you are on. Life is good; you don't have to wait until you reach the Promised Land to celebrate yourself and the life you are living.

7. **Avoid the Dream Stealers:** Unfortunately, just before you take your first step on the righteous journey to pursue your dreams, people around you, even the ones who deeply care for you, will give you awful advice. It's not because they have evil intentions. It's because they don't understand the big picture—what your dreams, passions, and life goals mean to you. They don't understand that, to you, the reward is worth the time and sacrifice. So they try to protect you by shielding you from the possibility of failure, which, in effect, also shields you from the possibility of making your dreams a reality.

   Some will say, "You can follow your dreams someday, but right now you need to buckle down and be responsible." Someday? When is "someday"? Someday is not a day at all. It's a foggy generalization of a time that will likely never come. Today is the only day you can begin to make a difference in your life. And pursuing your dreams is what life is all about. So don't be irresponsible. Don't wait until "someday." Make today the first day of the rest of your new life.

   Others will say, "That sounds like a lot of hard work. It's not worth the time." Yep, building a network marketing business is hard work all right. It may be the hardest work you ever do. But is it worth it? I think so. Success in life hinges on finding hard work you love doing. As long as you remain true to yourself and follow your own interests, values, and dreams, you can find success.

   What's the alternative? Waking up every day working in a career field you despise, wondering, "How the heck am I going to do this for the next twenty to thirty years?" So if you catch yourself working hard at building your network marketing business, and loving every minute of it, don't stop. You're on to something BIG.

Some people will even tell you that you're not good enough, or it's safer to keep doing what you're doing at your day job. Seriously? These people think they have your best interests in mind, but they really just don't want you to get ahead. Sorry for the reality check, but it's true. The reason being that if you get ahead, they'll feel bad about themselves because you have something they don't. That's their issue, not yours. Don't let someone else's baggage hold you back.

And then there is the friend or relative who suggests that you might fail, or worse yet, makes the comment, "Nobody makes money at those things; only the people at the top make all the money." You know what I have to say about that? They're right. If you think you are going to fail, you will. If you think you are going to succeed, you will. And if you want to make a lot of money in network marketing, then you do need to be at the top of your own business. And everyone entering a network marketing company has the opportunity to build it big and be at the top of his or her own organization. Your decision and mindset to succeed will make all the difference. Don't buy into anyone else's small way of thinking or let it deter you from thinking big and achieving your dreams.

If you haven't figured it out by now, I like to keep it real and transparent. There are a few obstacles you can expect when you take the journey to pursue your dreams via network marketing. First, there's that thing between your ears that will play tricks on you and make you question yourself. Yes, at times, you're going to be scared. It's only natural and I've experienced it myself. Fear may be paralyzing at times, but just remember that your desire and passion to do what you love has a stronger hold on you than fear ever can. Focus on the positive and why you're doing what you're doing.

There will be times when you may feel uncertain or uncomfortable. Chances are you will have to step way out of your comfort zone. A lot of this will be centered on your prospecting efforts and feelings toward facing rejection. Such feelings are only natural; I still face those challenges from time to time. I've found them to be a good thing because you're going to need to face those challenges in order to grow as a person and a leader.

Then there are the days when doubt will creep into your mind. This too is natural, but a sign that you need to work on your belief in yourself and your dream. You'll eventually learn either to laugh at your doubt and move past it, or spend way too much time entertaining it and making tons of meaning out of it when you could be chasing your dreams instead.

One thing is for certain, you're going to learn what you're made of. There will be times when you want to give up, when you question whether network marketing is for you. Eventually, you'll just decide to roll with it and know that it's part of the process. Rolling with it will end up being incredibly rewarding.

Think about the amazing leaders of the past who have changed the way we live our lives. What would life have been like for all of us today if they hadn't dreamt BIG?

**What would life be like if Thomas Edison or Henry Ford didn't follow their dreams as inventors?**

**What would our society be like if Martin Luther King, Jr. didn't follow his dream of equality?**

**What would your productivity be like if Bill Gates didn't pursue his dreams around software development and the personal computer?**

**Would you even be reading this book about network marketing if it were not for the dream Rich DeVos and Jay Van Andel had to found the Amway Corporation?**

The number of BIG Dreamers in our history is infinite. Take a moment and dream a little. In the section below, write out your dream, the sacrifices you're willing to make for it, and when you want to achieve it. (If you have more than one dream, great! Use a separate sheet of paper for each one).

**Exercise**

What's your dream?

_____
_____
_____
_____
_____
_____
_____
_____

When do you want to achieve your dream?

_____
_____
_____
_____
_____
_____
_____
_____
_____

What sacrifices are you willing to make to pursue that dream?

_____

_____

_____

_____

_____

_____

_____

_____

## CHAPTER 2

# HAVING THE PROPER MINDSET

"Whatever the mind can conceive and believe, it can achieve."

— Napoleon Hill

The way you think is going to dictate the distance you go with your business and life.

Have you ever looked at successful entrepreneurs and wondered what they did to become so successful? Several traits separate those high achievers from those who go through life settling for what life gives them. However, the number one trait that has made a huge difference in every successful entrepreneur's career is mindset.

Having the proper mindset is one of the most powerful resources available to any human being. Your mindset will affect everything in your life, including your relationships, physical and mental energy, stamina, self-image, work habits, ability to deal with adversity, overall happiness, and of course, your ability to succeed at building your network marketing business.

Over the years of my network marketing journey, I've watched people with average talents and a positive mindset triumph over the enormously talented person with a negative or unfocused mindset. Of all the physical and mental traits possessed by human beings, having the right mindset stands alone as the great divider between average performance and peak achievement.

You may be wondering what is the proper mindset needed to succeed in your network marketing business. There are actually three categories of mindset required:

1. The mindset of *success*
2. The mindset of an *entrepreneur*
3. The mindset of *gratitude*

You must focus on developing all three of these mindsets if you want to build your network marketing business. Therefore, let's look at each of these categories more closely.

## The Mindset of Success

From my perspective, it all starts with visualizing success and honoring the fact that you deserve it. Visualize what your life will be like when you succeed in business. What will you have that you don't have today? Where and how will you live? How many people could you help as a result of your success? Once you visualize the success you seek, you need to honor the fact that you deserve it. Erase any negative thoughts that you have regarding your upbringing or previous failed attempts at business. Just because you have not been successful in the past, or don't come from a lineage of entrepreneurs, doesn't mean you can't break the mold and become successful. It will take a shift in your attitude and mindset to set the stage for success. Begin with the end in mind.

**The Mindset of an Entrepreneur**

If you don't come to network marketing with an entrepreneurial background, you may need to shift your thoughts from an employee mindset to an entrepreneur mindset. Think about that one for a moment. Employees have the mindset that they need to go to work and conduct some activities, and then they will get paid at the end of the week. They are in their comfort zone because everything is predictable, including what their job description is, when they need to work, and how much they will get paid. When work is done, it's done.

Entrepreneurs, on the other hand, need to have a completely different mindset. They don't have a predictable paycheck, and they need to be critical thinkers, highly motivated, disciplined, proactive, and ultimately, control their own destinies. They may need to sacrifice family time, weekends, and even vacations to get to the level of success they are looking for. Is it worth it? Absolutely!

**The Mindset of Gratitude**

Another way to help you craft and maintain the proper mindset is a perspective of gratitude. In the world we live in, we are constantly bombarded with messages about what we don't have. People are comparing themselves to the "Joneses" next door rather than focusing on what matters. Although I've been guilty of this in the past, I do my best to wake up to abundance every day. Being grateful for what you do have will help you radiate a positive mental energy. Whom do people gravitate to at social gatherings? It's invariably the person with the positive outlook and enthusiastic attitude. People want to be around positive people with a bright outlook on life. Turn on your love light and leave it on! Be grateful for what you have. Believe that your success will only increase and you will find that you attract even more good into your life.

**Five Tips for Developing the Right Mindset**

Most top income earners in network marketing have mastered the right mindset to succeed in all three of the above categories. As part of my gratitude mindset, I believe in passing on what I have gained so others can have what I have. Therefore, here are my five top tips for developing a proper mindset to succeed in network marketing:

1. **Feel Good about Yourself:** How you feel about yourself has a major impact on your mindset. If you feel lazy, unmotivated, or out of shape, you won't respect yourself, and in turn, you won't have a positive mindset. Conversely, if you are in good shape, have confidence in what you are doing, know you are a person of integrity, and handle challenges with a solution in mind, then a positive mindset is a natural extension of this view of yourself. You have total control of your self-image and self-confidence. It may take some time, but feeling good about who you are and what you have to offer the world is a critical step in creating the success mindset.

2. **Exercise Regularly and Eat Clean:** The better physical shape you are in, the easier it is for you to feel good about yourself and what you are doing. When you are in good shape, you are more productive, and that leads to the proper expectations regarding what you will attract to your life and your business. Create a pattern of regular exercise. The effects of physical activity on the way you think can be profound. Find an activity, get passionate about it, and be consistent.

   As the saying goes, you are what you eat. Today's processed foods play a major role in the way our society thinks and acts. The chemicals injected into these foods are creating many diseases, including obesity, diabetes, cancer, and mental disorders. If you adopt a clean-eating lifestyle, your mental mindset and productivity will improve considerably.

3. **Learn from Others Who Have Achieved Success:** I already talked about the importance of finding a mentor and following those who have achieved success, but you don't always have to find someone to be your mentor in-person. You can also read books on successful entrepreneurs or listen to entrepreneur podcasts online that interview other successful entrepreneurs. These are great ways to get yourself into the correct mindset to succeed within your business. Hearing about other entrepreneurs' mistakes will help you avoid pitfalls others have already gone through and save you time and heartache down the road. Hearing about their successes will inspire you and give you a model to build from.

4. **Check Your Emotions at the Door:** Building a network marketing business can be very emotional. Friends and family will reject you, call you crazy, and silently root for you to fail. I know that sounds harsh, but it's true. You will set goals and not achieve them, have people be no shows for your home launch party, and get distracted by team members looking at other programs. All of this, and more, will create emotions that can sidetrack your success mindset. Now that you know these things will happen, prepare yourself for when they do. Roll with the punches and accept the path you're on, including all the objections and rejections that will inevitably happen along the way. Need to work on your emotions? Practice yoga, meditate first thing in the morning, or take a walk when things get a little crazy. These activities will help you create and maintain the positive mindset you need.

5. **Create a Personal Mission Statement:** Write a personal mission statement that spells out who you are and what you want your life to become. Keep it close at hand for regular review. When you are faced with a business challenge or setback, pull out your statement and remind yourself of the person you are

and the emotionally compelling vision you are working to achieve. Your personal mission statement will help you refocus on your ultimate destination and reconnect with your passion.

**Exercise**

Answer the following questions to help you create the proper mindset.

What do you love about yourself?

_____
_____
_____
_____
_____
_____
_____
_____
_____
_____

What are you committed to doing to improve your health and physical wellbeing?

_____
_____
_____
_____
_____
_____
_____
_____
_____
_____

What network marketing leader(s) do you admire who have had success?

_____
_____
_____
_____
_____

What emotions are you feeling around the thoughts of becoming successful with your business?

_____
_____
_____
_____
_____

What is your personal mission statement?

_____
_____
_____
_____
_____

What are you grateful for?

_____
_____
_____
_____
_____

## CHAPTER 3

# BUILDING BELIEF

"It's the repetition of affirmations that leads to belief. And once that belief becomes deep conviction, things begin to happen."

— Muhammad Ali

I'm a big sports fan, and one of my favorite athletes to watch over the years has been professional golfer Tiger Woods. Tiger turned professional at age twenty in the late summer of 1996. By April 1997, he had already won his first major tournament, the 1997 Masters, in a record-breaking performance, winning by twelve strokes. He reached the number one position in world rankings in June 1997. Through the 2000s, Tiger was the dominant force in golf, spending 545 weeks as the world's #1 player between August 1999 and October 2010. During that time, he won nearly 100 golf tournaments.

A lot of factors contributed to Tiger becoming a champion: the decision he made as a child to be a professional golfer, his willingness to be coachable, his commitment to the process, and his ability to fight through adversity. But the number one reason Tiger won was because he believed he was going to win. Week in and week out, for over a decade, Tiger would enter a tournament knowing he could win, and often, he knew he *would* win. And that, my friends, is the power of belief.

Belief will play a role in anything you are looking to accomplish in life. If you want to build a successful network marketing business, you will need to build your belief in five core areas:

1. The products you sell
2. The company you represent
3. The networking marketing profession
4. The team of people you are working with
5. Yourself

Each of these areas is vital to believe in. Let's look at why.

**Products**
Network marketing companies offer consumable products that are often unique and a higher quality than most brands you would find in retail stores. Whether the category is nutrition, weight loss, skin care, makeup, electric utilities, or any of dozens of other categories, the products are all sold with someone telling the story behind them, and that means you have to become a storyteller.

In order to tell that story effectively, you must believe in the product's value and the benefits it will provide. In my experience, the only way to get a customer is to be a satisfied one yourself. This requires you to consume the products your company offers and to become a raving fan. Your belief in the products will only go as far as the results you experience. If you have a positive experience or see the value in your product, you will be able to share it with others.

**Company**

Are the owners of the company you sell for trustworthy? Are the products delivered on time? Are they priced reasonably? Are the commission checks paid on time? Does the company have a mission and culture that you feel comfortable with? Is there a long-term vision?

The answers to these questions and others will dictate the level of belief you have in your company. In order to succeed in this business, your belief needs to be so high that you would never consider representing another company. The best way to build belief in your company is to attend its events. Being able to rub elbows with likeminded people, meet the company's owners and executives, and learn from its leaders are all benefits to attending events. From these experiences, you will be able to build your belief around the company you represent.

**The Network Marketing Profession**

When I enrolled in my first network marketing company, the opportunity was clear to me. I saw value in the product. The company seemed to have it together. When the circles were drawn out, I saw the money potential. But my belief level about network marketing as a profession was probably a 5 on a scale of 1-10.

At the time, I had just started a career in the financial services industry. I was afraid of what people would think of me if I presented them with a business opportunity or tried to save them money on their long distance bills. As a result, I never approached the best and brightest people I knew at the time. I kept my sales to close family and friends because I was afraid of what people would think of me being involved in "one of those things." I had no conviction behind what I was doing, and I really didn't know anyone personally who had succeeded with the network marketing business model. I was in it to make money, yes, but in no way did I envision the opportunity to make a career out it.

My lack of belief in the model of network marketing was one of the primary reasons why I didn't make any money the first four years I was in the business. In all honesty, it took me over ten years before I finally got my belief level high enough that I was able to feel confident that I was in the right business. But once I got it, it became much easier to talk to people about the opportunity of network marketing and the benefits it can provide.

If you are looking to build your belief in the profession of network marketing, I would like to suggest that you attend one of the three generic industry events that happen throughout the year. The three I attend are:

1.  Eric Worre's Go Pro Mastery Event: www.networkmarketingpro.com
2.  The Direct Selling Mastermind Event: www.mastermindevent.com
3.  The annual convention for the Association of Network Marketing Professionals: www.ANMP.com

At any of these events, you will have the opportunity to hear from people just like you who made a decision to build a networking business, and then achieved incredible success. Their stories will open your eyes to what could be, and ultimately, increase your belief to the level needed to succeed with your business.

**Your Team**
Network Marketing is a business. And in order for the average person to succeed, it helps to be part of a dynamic team of people who have business experience and your best interest in mind. For any relationship to flourish, it comes down to knowing, liking, and

trusting. Without a high level of trust between team members, it can be difficult to possess the belief necessary to build it big.

**Yourself**

You can have life-changing products, a lucrative compensation plan, a solid company to represent, an amazingly supportive team, and think that network marketing is the best thing since sliced bread. But if you don't believe in yourself and your ability to succeed, it's going to be an uphill battle. It's imperative that you believe that you deserve to make more money and live a better life. You must develop the self-confidence to step outside of the box and talk to more people. You must be humble enough to recognize that you may have to learn new skill sets to move your business forward. And none of this will happen if you allow that thing between your ears to wreak havoc with the way you think about yourself and your ability to succeed.

We all have self-doubt from time to time; it's only natural. But how you deal with it, or try to adjust it, is a whole different thing. The self-development industry is alive and well, and you should subscribe to it. Countless resources are out there for you to take advantage of. Self-help seminars, books, audio books, videos, and personal coaches are all abundant and readily available.

We are all a product of our upbringing and environment. While change is constant, the right change is what you are looking for. If your belief in yourself is not a 10 on the 1-10 scale, subscribe to a regular dose of personal development because your breakthrough could be right around the corner.

**Exercise**

Where is your belief on a scale of 1-10?

Products                    1 2 3 4 5 6 7 8 9 10

Company                   1 2 3 4 5 6 7 8 9 10

Network Marketing    1 2 3 4 5 6 7 8 9 10

Your Team                 1 2 3 4 5 6 7 8 9 10

Yourself                     1 2 3 4 5 6 7 8 9 10

What are you going to do to increase your belief in each of these categories?

_____

_____

_____

_____

_____

_____

_____

_____

_____

_____

_____

_____

_____

_____

_____

_____

## Chapter 4

# Making the Decision

"Using the power of decision gives you the capacity to get past any excuse to change any and every part of your life in an instant."

— Tony Robbins

This chapter is going to be short and to the point. You can be the biggest dreamer on the planet and possess the ultimate success mindset. Your belief levels can be a 10 out of 10 in your products, company, the network marketing profession, and yourself. But if you don't make the decision that you are going to build a successful network marketing business right now, it's not going to happen.

Over the years, I've watched countless people talk a good game. They talk about building it big. They claim to possess all the skill sets necessary to succeed. They show up at events and set goals. But they can't seem to get out of their own way because they have not made one simple *decision*—the decision that they are going to use the model of network marketing to achieve their dreams, goals, and aspirations.

In order to make that decision, you may need to overcome your limiting beliefs, you may need to become fearless in talking to people, and you may need to be forever dedicated to working on yourself and helping others do the same.

There are two major reasons why people fail to make that decision:

1.  **Procrastination:** That "someday" mindset that suggests you will get around to it, or you are too busy, or you don't have the money are just excuses. I have to admit I've had a tendency to procrastinate in my day. The good news is that I've felt the pain of procrastination and then learned that making a decision was better and more productive.

2.  **Fear:** Fear is a natural feeling that many people have when they embark on a new endeavor. People fear what people will think, they fear rejection, they fear failure, and believe it or not, some people fear success. The only way to address the fear you may have is to face it head on.

When I was a kid, I had a fear of diving off the high diving board at our community pool. I can remember climbing the ladder and standing at the edge of the diving board frozen in time. My mother would stand poolside, encouraging me to jump. I can remember not having the guts to jump and retreating down the stairs. I did this several times before going to the pool one day determined to jump. To this day, I can remember when I jumped. It was terrifying, but I lived. And once I did it, I wanted to do it again, and again. I overcame my fears with that initial jump and plunge into the deep end. The same applies to all the fears you may have with your business. Once you take action, fall down, and pick yourself up, your confidence will build and you'll become unstoppable.

Life has decisions at every turn. A couple of years ago, I was faced with re-evaluating my life as I knew it. I have lived a good life and was grateful for what I had, but I was thinking about how I could improve it. I made the following three decisions that offered both instant and future gratification:

1. **Live for today:** Life is short. Wake up each morning and be grateful to be alive. Follow your passions. Do something for yourself each and every day because you deserve it! No regrets.

2. **Save for tomorrow:** One of the biggest challenges people have today is they have not saved enough for retirement. If you're a baby boomer, maybe you can relate. It may even be the reason why you're building a network marketing business. If you're a millennial, saving for retirement is probably the last thing on your mind. But if you need a wakeup call or reminder of what a challenge it could be, look at your parents or your friends' parents. Paying yourself first and being frugal is actually cool. Ask anyone who is living a comfortable retirement today based on a decision he or she made years ago.

   Don't get caught up in the mindset of needing a fancy car, an expensive watch, or a big house to feel accomplished. I'm so passionate about this subject that I'm already planning a book on personal finance for network marketers. Make a decision to save for tomorrow. It's really important!

3. **Take action now:** Here is where the rubber meets the road. Make the decision that network marketing is going to be your vehicle for achieving your dreams. Once you've made that decision, you need to take the necessary action to build your business. And not just any action—income-producing action. I'll talk more about this in the next section.

**Exercise**

Take a moment and think about some of the decisions you have made in your life.

What are some of the decisions you have made in the past that you regret?

_____

_____

_____

_____

_____

What did you learn from those decisions?

_____

_____

_____

_____

_____

What are some of the decisions you have made that ended up being positive and rewarding?

_____

_____

_____

_____

_____

How did those positive decisions improve your life?

_____

_____

_____

_____

_____

As it pertains to your network marketing business, what are some of the decisions you have procrastinated on or have flat out avoided?

_____

_____

_____

_____

_____

Why have you not made the decision? When are you going to make it?

_____

_____

_____

_____

_____

# PART II

# TAKING ACTION

"Action is the foundational key to all success."

— Pablo Picasso

In the previous section, I addressed the importance of dreaming big, getting the proper mindset, building belief, and making a decision. Over the years, I have been involved with people who were great at the mental game. They had big dreams, were positive, believed in what they were doing, and even made a decision to build a business.

The thing they were missing was taking the action necessary to build the business. They never got out of the gate because they had a challenge creating the necessary ripples to get their business off the ground. Network marketing is an interesting business because of the fact that it is both easy to do and easy not to do. Therefore, it is important that you know what actions are important to building your business.

In this next section, I'm going to focus on what I feel are some of the key "taking action" principles or concepts you need to implement in building your business. I learned these principles over the years, and they served as the baseline of building a solid foundation with my business. If you apply these principles to your business, you will increase the probability of not only succeeding, but creating a following of people who emulate these critical and necessary ripple-creating actions.

## CHAPTER 5

# LAUNCHING YOUR BUSINESS

"Twenty years from now you will be more disappointed by the things that you didn't do than by the ones you did do. So throw off the bowlines. Sail away from the safe harbor. Catch the trade winds in your sails. Explore. Dream. Discover."

— Mark Twain

One of the common mistakes I see people make when trying to build a business in network marketing is that they don't give the business the respect it deserves. You have probably heard the saying, "Treat it like a hobby, and it will cost you money; treat it like a business, and it can make you money." Well, it's true; if you want to build a legitimate and profitable business, you need to treat your little home-based business like the multi-million-dollar opportunity it is.

**Go Public**

I have a friend who invested hundreds of thousands of dollars in a franchise. He leveraged everything he owned to start that business, and when it came time to open the doors, he did it with major fanfare. He placed advertisements in all sorts of media to announce his new business, had a grand opening celebration, and offered the public all kinds of promotional items for showing up to see what he had to offer. He wasn't just starting his business, he was launching it to the community, and he wanted to let everyone know it existed.

When you look to engage in your network marketing business, it should be no different. Do not start your business, *launch it!* Treat it as if you invested a million dollars into it, not $500. The best and only way to do it properly is to go public and let people know what you are doing, why you are doing it, and what you are looking for.

Don't worry about what people will think, or whether they will buy your product. You want to be excited about what you are doing and what you have to offer. If you're not excited, why would anyone else be? When it comes to going public, it's all a function of belief. If there's anyone you know whom you are hesitant to approach, then your belief level is not high enough. If that's the case, you have some work to do.

Multiple ways exist for effectively launching your business, but they all entail talking to a lot of people. Some network marketers host a series of home launch parties. Others direct people to conference calls or websites to get the information. Still others use social media and other marketing tools to make people aware. Regardless of the approach or tools you use, the key is talking to people, having conversations about their needs, finding their pain, and putting yourself in a situation to provide them with a solution.

### Create Personal Momentum
Whether you are just getting started or looking to re-launch your business, your primary goal is to create what I call "personal momentum." In other words, you want to engage in the right activities and create enough energy to set the business growth in motion.

To create this personal momentum, you'll want to acquire a bunch of customers, create interest in the business, and ultimately develop some business volume that will start your advancement through the compensation plan. This process requires contacting a lot of people within a short period of time and having a grand opening of sorts. You can't be shy with whom you approach; everyone you know should be on your candidate list.

When you approach people, whether you lead with the product or the business will depend on your personality, influence, experience, and the company you represent. I've always felt that a combination of product and business is best. If you have a great product to share with people and it has value, you should be proud to present what you have. At the same time, people today, more than ever, are looking to change their financial situations as well, so don't shortchange yourself by just talking about the product offering and not also talking about how network marketing works with your company and the benefits it can also offer them (which will benefit you by extension if they become involved).

Never prejudge someone based on what you think his or her interest may be. I've always advised people to go to the best and brightest people they know with the business model. Successful people tend to get it, and when they do, they take action like the best of them. The same applies to your product offering. Don't assume anything when it comes to interest in what you have to offer. To create the personal momentum you are looking for takes a special course of action steps, and there is no better time than the first ninety days of launching your business for taking those steps.

**Develop a Ninety-Day Campaign**
I've always told people that it's easier to build fast than to build slow. Think about that for a moment. What's more exciting? Watching a fast-paced sporting event, or watching paint dry?

I've observed a lot of people in this business over the years. I've studied those who succeed as well as those who don't. One of the core reasons why some people don't reach their goals is they only get around to talking to people about their product or business when it's convenient to them. In other words, they are not consistent with their actions and approaching people every day. Pardon the bluntness, but that dog won't hunt. In order to launch your business effectively, or create some momentum in your business, you need to commit to a ninety-day campaign.

A ninety-day campaign is a personal commitment to talk to people consistently about your business and products every day for ninety days. I'm talking all-out-massive action with a focus on building your business and attracting people to what you have to offer.

Your overall focus should be on advancing through your compensation plan. In every compensation plan, there is that foundational rank or position that is the first step in advancing through your plan. Know what it is and what you have to do to achieve it. Advance to that position as quickly as possible, and help others to do the same.

To have an effective campaign, you will need to sacrifice some things in your life. Maybe less time with friends, not watching TV, taking a break from playing golf, or some other activities you enjoy. These sacrifices aren't forever; just for the period of time it takes for you to create the business volume you need to create a business story worth telling.

**An Amazing Story of Launching a Business**
Let me give you a real life story of how I effectively helped my friend and business partner launch her business—and create massive results. When I enrolled my friend Brandy into our business, she wanted to build fast. She lived on the island of Oahu. Our com-

pany had no leaders in Hawaii, so she saw not only the value in the products and what they could do for her community, but the opportunity to be the first to develop the market.

After we talked about the goals she had, we decided that our efforts would be centered around a ninety-day campaign—a campaign driven by the results people were having with the product, and the opportunity to help others build a business of their own.

The campaign started by getting as many people as possible to try the products during the campaign's first thirty days so we could develop a lot of success stories. In the process, we attracted a handful of people who not only saw the value in the products, but who also loved the idea of sharing with others and creating a secondary stream of income.

For the second thirty days, we focused on doing as many in-home presentations as possible. To do this effectively, I flew to Oahu for the month and taught Brandy and her team the concept of personal in-home meetings, and how if they are done effectively, you can create a ground swell of activity and a lot of excitement around the opportunity.

It all started in her mom's home where we invited as many people as we could to tell the story and show the plan to. At the end of that presentation, we told everyone that we were doing the same presentation the following night, but they could come back only if they brought a guest. The following evening, we had twice as many people and the enrollments and excitement started to swell. We were not only enrolling new customers, but also people who wanted to share the products. We offered to do the same presentation in their homes, so we literally went from living room to living room, spreading the word about the life-changing products and opportunity we had for anyone who was interested.

Within ten days, we outgrew the capacity of living rooms and promoted an event at the local country club. At that event, we had over 100 people in attendance sharing their product stories and how they were making money with the business. Every day, all day, for thirty days, we got in front of people to tell the story of what we had to offer and how they could participate. Whether it was in a living room, at a Starbucks, in a hotel lobby, or on the beach, we told the same story and used the same tools over and over again. By the end of the campaign's first sixty days, we had a training event in which over 200 people attended to learn how they, too, could effectively build a business.

It was a magical launch for Brandy's business, and I can't count how many lives have been changed as a result of the efforts.

One of the key factors in this business's successful launch was that we never ended an event without promoting the next one. We created a sense of urgency with the team we were building by continually focusing on the next event and what these products would do for the community. Brandy subscribed to the concept of a ninety-day campaign, and the results were amazing. Over a thousand people were enrolled, she attracted many satisfied loyal customers, and she found some individuals who wanted to partner with her in her business. She created some serious personal momentum, and as a result, she earned over a million dollars in her business within the subsequent two years. That financial success was 100 percent attributed to the principle of conducting a ninety-day campaign.

Now these results don't happen everywhere, but this story is a classic example of what can happen when you make a decision to do something, have the proper mindset, and take the right action centered on a specific plan.

So if you are a new distributor in your company, take this story to heart. Make a decision that you want to build it huge and create a plan for a ninety-day campaign of your own to launch your business and create personal momentum for yourself and your initial team members.

If you are already engaged in your business, but not experiencing the growth you want, you should relaunch your business with a ninety-day campaign of your own. All you have to do is make a decision, set the goals, and take massive action. All activities should be income-producing, and staying consistent will be the key to your success. As the Nike slogan says, "Just do it!"

**Exercise**

Your Ninety-Day Campaign

To help you set the tone for the launch or re-launch of your business, answer the following:

What is your starting date?  _____

How big is your list?  _____

How will you be inviting people from your list?  _____

How many invitations will you make per day?  _____

How many presentations will you make per day?  _____

What is your rank advancement goal?  _____

What is your personal enrollment goal?  _____

What events are you promoting into?  _____

Do your team members have the answers to these questions as well?   Y/N

## CHAPTER 6

# DESIGNING YOUR DMO
## (DAILY METHOD OF OPERATION)

"The successful warrior is the average man, with laser-like focus."

— Bruce Lee

Most people who are involved in network marketing are doing so on a part-time basis. They are working a full-time job or running another traditional business and spending between five and twenty hours per week on building their business. To be effective in business, whether you are part-time or full-time, you need a daily method of operation (DMO). What this means is that the time you have to spend on building your business needs to be organized, and on purpose.

**Blocking Out Time**
Regardless of the time you spend on building your business, you want to be productive. When I started in network marketing, I had a career working as a financial advisor. My days were dedicated to building another business, so the only time I had to focus on my

network marketing business was in the evening or on the weekend.

This brings me to the main point of blocking out time. You are going to have to sacrifice if you are interested in making this work. You may have to pass on one of those weekend activities with friends to attend that Saturday training event. Or maybe you need to make prospecting calls at night instead of watching your favorite TV show. Speaking of which, there is no BV (business volume) in TV, so pass the remote already.

**Income-Producing Activities (IPAs)**
Once you plan out the schedule of when you will be working on your business, the key is what you do with your time. One of my biggest challenges early in my career was what I called being in "project mode" or spending time on "busy work." It seemed like the majority of my time I was either trying to create a better presentation or training, brainstorming with other distributors about an event we could do and what we would present, or building a "better" website than what the company had provided. Or worse yet, I would spend time with unproductive distributors, thinking they would do something they were not capable of doing. Looking back on those countless hours that I will never get back, it's clear to me that it was totally wasted time—and all an excuse not to pick up the phone and call someone about my product or opportunity.

If you are new to your network marketing opportunity, you have not reached your financial goals, or you don't have a consistent monthly check with one or two digits in front of a comma, you need to be focusing the majority of your time on income-producing activities (IPAs). In case you're wondering what defines an IPA, it's an activity that produces income that goes into your bank account. Listening to conference calls, reading about your products online, reading that personal development book, watching that video online, or spending meaningless hours scrolling through your Facebook feed do not count as IPAs. You want to focus on activities such as:

- Prospecting for new distributors and customers
- Inviting people to watch your video presentation
- Calling customers and asking for referrals
- Getting your newest distributors started right
- Conducting three-way or connect calls
- Attending a training event with your team
- Building relationships with Facebook friends
- Following up and asking for the order

Like any business, you have to create business volume to get paid. Network marketing is no different; the more business volume you create, the more money you will make. The goal is to build a team of motivated and committed distributors who all focus on sharing with everyone they know.

**Exercise**

Create your personal Daily Method of Operation

How many hours per week will you work on your business?

I will work my business on these days at these hours:

Monday          _____

Tuesday         _____

Wednesday       _____

Thursday        _____

Friday          _____

Saturday        _____

Sunday          _____

I am committed to contacting _____ people per day about my opportunity or product offering.

I will plug into my team and training calls as follows:

Day                          Time

_____          _____

_____          _____

_____          _____

_____          _____

_____          _____

_____          _____

## CHAPTER 7

# DUPLICATING WITH A SYSTEM

"Getting an audience is hard. Sustaining an audience is hard. It demands a consistency of thought, of purpose, and of action over a long period of time."

— Bruce Springsteen

For years, franchising has been one of the more popular options for people looking to start a business. When people invest into a franchise, they are buying into the experience and goodwill created by the entrepreneurs who created the concept. This investment includes the ability to buy into a brand name with a proven track record. In addition to a well-known brand name, buying a franchise offers many other advantages that aren't available to the entrepreneur starting a business from scratch. Perhaps the most significant is that you get a proven system of operation and training on how to build the business. As a result, new franchisees can avoid a lot of the mistakes start-up entrepreneurs typically make because the franchisor has already perfected daily operations through trial and error. The systems created within the franchise model are the backbone of what is most important for success: duplication.

I have always looked at network marketing as the "franchise without the franchise fee"—the reason being that in order to succeed in network marketing, you have to have a proven system that the average person can duplicate. The key word here is *duplicate*.

Over the years, I've watched hundreds of high quality people come into network marketing with all kinds of ideas. Some would create their own websites so they could tell the story the way they thought it should be told. Others would come from the health and wellness industry, so they would want to target doctors and other medical practitioners. Still others would come to the table with great backgrounds and skill sets in Internet marketing and other business practices.

All these people would try to implement unique ways in which they were going to market the business, determine vertical markets they were going to target, and create "prospecting systems" to generate leads for them. The problem wasn't their passion for building a business; it was that the ideas and strategies they wanted to implement could work for them, but they wouldn't duplicate into an organization.

There's a saying I've used over the years, and it's the moral of this chapter: "It's not what works; it's what duplicates." In network marketing, it all starts with you and everything you do.

Following are just a few of the key parts of building a business that you want to see duplicate:

- What products you consume and how you present them to prospects
- The story of your company, and how you tell it
- What you say to prospects to get their attention and interest

- How you enroll new customers and distributors
- What tools to use, and how to use them
- The training systems your team follows to get started

Think about this for a minute. Is everyone in your company or organization telling the story the same way? Is everyone using the same tools? When people are enrolled, do they all start with the same product offering? Are the "getting started" trainings offering the same message? If the answer to any of these questions is "No," I'm willing to bet there is confusion in the field and your business is not growing as much as it could be.

The solution to having "franchise-like" duplication starts at the top. Field leaders need to be congruent in all aspects of the business if they want their organizations to grow to their full potential. When field leaders are on the same page by pitching the same story, selling the same program, using the same tools, promoting the same campaign, and offering the same basic getting started training, magical things can happen.

**The Power of Duplication**
In 1999, I became a founding distributor for a company offering health and wellness products. The company had a product that produced results, a way to measure those results, and a marketing tool to tell the story. We took these three core items and packaged them into a system that would duplicate and build an organization.

Our pitch was simple: "Our product will make you younger; we have a test that will prove it, and a tape that will sell it." (For all you millennials reading this, there was a thing called an audio cassette that came after the 8-track tape and before the CD.)

Everyone was looking for the fountain of youth. A test that could show that your biomarkers of aging were improving would certainly validate the product results. And all one had to do was hand out a twenty-five-cent audio cassette to sell it. It worked great! Everyone in the field was telling the same story, and it became a game of whoever handed out the most audio cassettes would win. When people enrolled, they all purchased the same package, and the same product was put on autoship. The training was very easy because the method of operation was as simple as using a powerful and effective tool. Nobody was making himself the issue; everyone could just let the tool do the presenting for him. Tens of thousands of cassettes were handed out and mailed through a fulfillment center, and we built an organization that went from zero to $2 million a month in sales in a pretty short period of time. This is a classic example of the power of duplication and how a system can attract people to your business. Keep it simple, and make it duplicable, and you will attract people to your business.

This brings me to the most important part of creating duplication: getting people started. When a new distributor enters your organization, how are you going to get that person started? Is there a standardized training for him to go through? Are you conducting a business planning session with her to get a feel for her goals, dreams, and why she is building a business? Do you provide him with the tools necessary to make his initial exposures and acquire initial customers and business partners? These are just a few of the questions you need to ask yourself if you want to see duplication in your business.

## High-Tech vs. High-Touch
Systems for building a network marketing business come in all shapes and sizes. Today, they tend to be a combination of high-tech and high-touch. The high-tech part of the equation lends itself to on-demand texting services, online funnels, phone apps, and social media.

People today are so attached to their smart phones that you really need to have a part of your system going through one's phone, especially for millennials. The communication trends today are centered on sending someone a text, having someone watch a video, sending an email, or tagging someone into a Facebook group. These forms of contacting people are very effective and can speed up the pace of moving one to and through the information.

The future of building a network marketing clientele is going to be driven through apps on your phone. You will use the apps to prospect people, place orders, manage your business, and much more. If your company doesn't have an effective phone app to help you build your business, you should have a discussion with your company owners.

On the other end of the spectrum is the high-touch aspect of your system. Examples of high touch include in-home meetings, one on ones, public business briefings, and handing out samples. Many people seem to feel that these high-touch ways of presenting your product or opportunity are "old school." However, I feel they are a significant part of the process. Remember, people buy people, not products. Being personable in the process is important. As far as relationship building is concerned, nothing beats the "belly-to-belly" atmosphere. You can bring people in via high tech, but it's the high touch that will enable you to build and enhance the relationship necessary for building a business that will last a lifetime.

### Let the Tools Do the Talking

One of the best pieces of advice I offer network marketers is not to make themselves the issue when building their businesses. By this, I mean that when you are talking to people about your product or opportunity, don't talk too much. Most amateur networkers talk their way right out of the chance to get a customer or business builder. They feel they need to explain everything about the product and what it will do for the customer. Or they tell prospects how much money they can make, when they have not made anything for themselves. This happens because you are so excited about what you've found that you want to share it with everyone you know, but to the prospect, it looks and feels like "word vomit."

Your job is to do nothing more than pique the interest of your prospect with respect to his or her interest in your product or opportunity. Once the prospect has been qualified and has expressed sincere interest in learning more, then you can point him to your favorite and most effective marketing tool. Tools come in many forms. The most popularly used tools include:

- Videos
- Websites
- Brochures
- Third-Party Publications
- Texting Services
- Phone Apps
- Public Presentations
- Product Samples
- Webinars
- Conference Calls
- Private Facebook Groups
- Three-Way Calls

Personally, I like to have multiple tools at my disposal. Some people like to read their information while others like to watch a video. Some like to see full presentations while others want to operate exclusively from their phones.

Regardless of what your story is, your company needs to have tools that will effectively tell the story and show the plan on your behalf. Your company either needs to create those tools in-house or out-source their production to a company that specializes in creating marketing tools for the network marketing industry. I've always used Sound Concepts for our marketing tools. Based out of American Fork Utah, Sound Concepts is the industry leader in marketing solutions for network marketing companies, and it is world class.

I hope you see the importance of creating, following, and ultimately, teaching a system to build your business. Whether it's high-touch, hi-tech, or a combination of both, the key is for it to be effective and duplicable throughout your organization.

**Exercise**

What are your go-to marketing tools for presenting your product or business?

_____

_____

_____

_____

_____

_____

What do you and your team have in place for getting new distributors started right?

_____

_____

_____

_____

_____

_____

How are you using high-tech vs. high-touch with your prospecting and business building system?

_____

_____

_____

_____

_____

_____

CHAPTER 8

# ATTENDING AND PROMOTING EVENTS

*"If you really look closely, most overnight successes took a long time."*

— Steve Jobs

When people ask me how I became successful in network marketing, I let them know it didn't come fast or easy. As a matter of fact, I barely covered my expenses during the first four years of trying to build a network. Friends and family members questioned what I was doing, and many told me I was wasting my time. At times, it seemed as if they were right, and I had periods of self-doubt. At times, it seemed like I couldn't get out of my own way, and the pressure was forcing me to look for the shortcut to success. The reality is there was no shortcut.

To better my chances of success, I became a student of the profession and ultimately acquired the skill sets to build a successful business. I built up my monthly check to $10,000 to $12,000 per month, which was great, but I was having trouble taking it to the next level. Something was missing, so I needed a mentor to help guide me.

Interestingly enough, that mentor emerged from within my organization. His name was John, and he was a successful network marketer. He had spent years with the Amway organization as a Diamond leader, so he came to our company with all kinds of experience in building high-performance teams. I can remember how excited I was when he came into the organization. When we first met, I got the opportunity to ask him about what drove his success in his previous endeavors. In replying, he didn't hesitate for a second. He told me that if I wanted to build a huge business in network marketing, I would have to get my head around the importance of events, and how the degree to which I promoted them would make all the difference in the world.

**Local Business Briefings**
When I asked John to define "events," he said they consisted of any gathering of people that moved your business forward. I learned the phrase "Build local and think global" from John. He explained that the most important thing you could do when launching your business was to build a local team and create an event structure in your backyard. These events consisted of a regularly scheduled local opportunity meeting where people could take a first look at the business. Home parties designed to launch one's business also fell into the local event category. He explained that the weekly local opportunity meetings and home parties were the baseline of the event structure and were designed to give people their first look at the business and create enrollments. Anyone who has done a series of home events or local meetings knows the power of these events.

I know some of you reading this think that face-to-face meetings are old school. You think you can build a business in your pajamas while working from home online or through social media and conference calls. Yes, those are significant ways to get people interested in what you have to offer, but using technology exclusively is not going to build you a business that will last a lifetime. You may be able to enroll a lot of people via high-tech means, but if you want to move them forward, you need to get connected with them at a larger public event.

**Regional Training Events**
This discussion brings us to the next level of events designed to help people see the bigger picture. These events are called everything from Super Saturdays to Regionals. They are usually all-day events that include a training component and recognition. Sometimes they are supported by the corporation, but usually, they are created and driven by the field leaders building that local area or region. I've seen them structured in different ways, but a price is usually associated with them so tickets need to be purchased.

John taught me one of my first big lessons about these types of events: *Never end an event without promoting the next event.* When John first brought this event structure to our company, I would purchase a ticket and attend. I would also tell the people in my organization to purchase a ticket and attend. Some did, and some didn't. Then John taught me that at the end of each event, you need to promote and offer tickets to the next event. The tickets would be offered in quantity discounts. For example, tickets might be $35 at the door, $25 in advance, or a block of ten tickets for $100. By creating these discounts, most people would buy in blocks. And because they bought in blocks, they would end up with more guests and newly enrolled distributors at the event than they would have if they had just bought their own tickets and told others to do the same. As a result, their businesses grew more coming out of the event.

Well, once I learned this and duplicated it in our organization, the attendance skyrocketed. At one event, I had 4,000 people on my team in attendance. As you can imagine, awesome things happened after that event.

**Annual Convention**

And then there is your company's annual convention. This is a destination event that usually lasts for two or three days. Conventions require a more significant investment because of the travel, hotels, and meals, but man, are they worth it.

I honestly don't know how anyone could not attend his or her company's annual convention. Local events bring people in; regional events move people along, but annual events teach people the skills they need to succeed, build unshakable belief, and develop the confidence necessary to win. Along with that comes the ability to build relationships with your team members, rub elbows with the top income earners, and experience the inspiration and motivation necessary to take your business to the next level. Those who attend their companies' national conventions see growth in their businesses afterwards. Those who attend with a team of people see significant growth.

You'll find that people who attend their annual conventions position themselves to make life-changing decisions. At these events, people make up their minds to make the profession of network marketing the focus of their careers, and they set big goals of achieving high ranks within their companies. All of these decisions are facilitated by high levels of energy, heavy attendance, and social proof provided by hearing others' success stories.

At annual conventions, companies offer all kinds of value, including:

- **Success Stories and Recognition:** These stories will inspire people and build belief with all attendees.

- **Product Training:** The distributor who understands the products will consume and sell more products.

- **Basic Business-Building Skills:** These are the basic skills people need to be more effective at building their businesses. They include your company's systematic approach to inviting, presenting, and enrolling new customers and distributors.

- **Leadership Development:** This is a big one. In order for a company to grow, the people must grow.

- **A Campaign:** At the end of every major event, there needs to be a campaign or game plan for the entire field to follow. Usually, it should be a 90-120 day campaign that will lead into a series of regionals events down the road.

### 1/3 Before, 1/3 At, 1/3 After

When it come to events, your primary goal is not to create momentum, but to advance it. And in order to have this happen, you will need to focus on what you do before the event, what you do at the event, and what you do after the event. Each of these phases plays a critical role in a successful event. How much you promote the event to your team and the number of people you have attending will bring energy and potential to the event. The content and execution of the event will dictate its effectiveness and the mindset created for the attendees. And the campaign and what you do after the event will dictate the level of activity, sales volume, and team building you experience.

### Become the Ultimate Promoter

As network marketers, we are in the people business, and events drive people. You can't simply announce the events and expect your people to register. You have to promote them. When events are announced, be the first to register, and tell everyone that you are going. Sell people on the value of the events by highlighting what will happen to their businesses if they attend. Get in the ticket-selling business and measure your success by the number of team members you have in attendance. Yes, you will have resistance from people who don't understand the value and suggest that they can't afford to attend. But it is your job to explain to them that this is not an expense; it is an investment in their future success. And the price of success is paid in advance.

**Exercise**

Think of three ways you can promote your upcoming events:

1. _____

2. _____

3. _____

## CHAPTER 9

# MARKETING ON SOCIAL MEDIA

"Everything you post on social media impacts your personal
brand. How do you want to be known?"

— David Skultety

I'm showing my age with this comment, but when I first got involved with network marketing there was no Internet, let alone
Facebook or any of the other social media platforms available today. We were dependent on the local weekly business briefing or
home party launch to expose people to our business. It was fun,
personable, and it worked.

Today, with the Internet and social media, the speed of making
an exposure and reaching out to people is amazing. You can alert
people to what you are doing and expose people around the world
with a simple push of the post button. Social media has completely transformed the way we communicate, build relationships, and
conduct business.

For anyone interested in building a network marketing business today, incorporating social media into your marketing strategy is a must. I caution you, however—especially if you're a millennial—that social media is only part, albeit a significant part, of your marketing mix. Public events will always play a significant role in building your business, so don't think you can build a business exclusively online and not have to get belly to belly at some point.

Network marketers who understand the power of social media and how to use it reap many benefits, including:

- Attracting new customers and business partners
- Building their personal brands
- Generating leads
- Enhancing relationships
- Developing a loyal following
- Communicating with their teams
- Recognition
- Creating culture and community
- And much more…

Network marketing is a business that succeeds primarily because of the person-to-person element. The real-life human touch of face-to-face conversations and activity is key to its success. For that reason, it's important to emphasize that social media is not the ultimate end-all in building your business; instead, you should think of it as a powerful tool to 1) attract a much wider audience, and 2) get that audience interested in who you are and what you are doing. Ultimately, you want your audience to get to know you, like you, and trust you. Once you have achieved that, you can take it from online to offline.

Many books and online programs can teach you how to use social media effectively to build your business, so for the purpose of this topic, I'm going to focus on seven Dos and four Don'ts of using social media to build your business.

**Do:**

1. **Choose the proper photo for your profile picture:** Think about the image you are trying to portray. This could be the first "visual" your audience has of you. This is the image that will appear anytime you comment, respond to, or share another's post. Be professional and don't use a picture of your cat.

2. **Provide valuable content:** Anything that inspires, educates, or entertains works best. Keep it real, raw, and genuine. People will buy into your authenticity vs. the persona you are trying to create.

3. **Be professional:** You want to project an image of someone who is trustworthy, dependable, and professional. Make sure all your content and interaction with others online maintains that image.

4. **Mind your manners:** When you first meet someone on social media, send that person a quick note to thank him or her for the connection. A simple acknowledgment and sign of sincere appreciation will go a long way toward building a relationship.

5. **Use videos to get your message out:** Video is what it's all about today. People want to be inspired, educated, and entertained, and there is no better way than doing live Facebook videos.

6. **Create engagement and interact with others:** Interact with people, like posts, compliment others. This will enhance relationships and get people to reciprocate.

7. **Personal message people on their birthdays:** This personal touch will go a long way.

**Don't:**

1. **Be an advertisement for your company or products:** This is the biggest mistake I see network marketers doing on social media. Once you post your products and company information online, you have created a wall between you and your friend. They will look at it the first time you post out of curiosity, and then chalk it up as ongoing white noise. If they are remotely interested, they will google to learn more and make a decision before you even speak to them.

2. **Post political, religious, or controversial topics:** You are entitled to your opinions and beliefs, but just look what happened during the most recent Presidential election. More relationships were tarnished due to political posts than any other subject since the introduction of the Internet.

3. **Inactivity:** If you are trying to create a following, build your personal brand, or attract people to what you are doing, you need to be seen. As with everything else in this business, be consistent with your posts.

4. **Spend too much time on social media:** It is very easy to get caught up in all the information that social media has to offer, but if you spend too much time scrolling through your feed, you're limiting the time you could be spending talking to people and building your business.

**Using Private Facebook Groups**

Another aspect of using social media to build your network marketing business is creating and participating in private Facebook groups. I have used private groups in three distinct ways:

1. **Prospecting Group:** When someone shows interest in your product or business, it is of great value if you have a private group you can add him or her to. Within these groups, you can have videos, business and product testimonials, and other content that will help your prospect through the evaluation process. This type of group could play an important role in your prospecting system.

2. **Product Group:** A private product page can be set up for customers of your products. This is a great forum for answering questions, introducing people to other products, and retaining customers.

3. **Business Builder Group:** This type of group provides a terrific forum of support, training, communication, recognition, and encouragement for those engaged in building a business.

Groups are only as good as their leaders. When done right, they can be a very powerful tool in advancing your business. Be sure to welcome new members, recognize success, interact with your team members, and make people feel at home. And use your groups to create the culture and community you want to instill in your business.

Remember, people don't join companies; they join people. Social media can play a significant role in helping you build a successful business.

**Exercise**

Find top-performing network marketers in your company or outside your company. Look them up on social media. Then given the points made above, determine:

What are they doing right on social media?

_____

_____

_____

_____

_____

What are they doing wrong on social media?

_____

_____

_____

_____

_____

Based on what I have learned, what changes can I make to my own social media presence to improve my network marketing strategies online?

_____

_____

_____

_____

_____

## CHAPTER 10

# TELLING STORIES

"Network marketing gives you the opportunity to face your fears, deal with them, overcome them, and bring out the winner that you have living inside you."

— Robert Kiyosaki

You may have heard the saying, "Facts tell, stories sell." Well, in network marketing, telling stories is the most powerful tool you will have at your disposal. Brochures, videos, and websites are all tools that play a part in attracting people to your business or product, but the stories you tell about what people are experiencing are what really captivate others and compel them to take action.

Everywhere you go when building your business, you will need to be able to tell stories. Whether you are at your weekly business briefing, on Facebook, at a one-on-one presentation, at a home launch party, conducting a three-way call, or on stage at your national convention, being able to tell an effective and relatable story is critical for your success.

When it comes to stories, there are two main storytelling techniques you want to master:

1. Highlighting your product or service's benefits or value.
2. Telling your business story.

Let's look in-depth at why these techniques are so important.

**Product Benefits and Value**
When describing your product's benefits and value, you want to connect with your prospective customer by being relatable and driving emotion. How the product makes you feel, what problem it has solved, and how it may have changed your life are all relatable aspects that drive emotion. People purchase products based on benefits, not the ingredients or science behind the product.

I once represented a company that formulated and manufactured scientific-based nutritional products. It used to drive me crazy how the company and distributors tried to be scientists and explain to people how the proprietary ingredients would affect them at the cellular level. All these scientific facts may have been true, but the average person cannot relate because, like me, most people didn't enjoy their chemistry or biology courses in high school. Most of the distributors wondered why their efforts didn't duplicate. It's because they focused on the science rather than keeping it simple by telling the amazing stories and benefits that the products produced.

**Your Business Story**
When telling your business story, it's never about how much money you have made; it's about how selling your product has changed your lifestyle and the lifestyles of others in your company. Telling people how your network marketing business has helped you eliminate your credit card debt, provided additional retirement

income, or afforded you the opportunity to take your family on vacation to Hawaii all create more curiosity and emotion than telling people you are making an extra $700 per month. Other examples of lifestyle benefits include not having to fight rush hour traffic, being able to stay home with your kids, having time to be present at your children's school events, and not having to wake up until you have finished sleeping. Today, people are longing for a better lifestyle more than anything, and network marketing is a vehicle that can provide that and more.

Following are three types of stories you can tell when talking to people about your opportunity or product offering:

**Your Upline's Story**
When you first get started in your business, you may not have a business or product story to tell others. As a result, you should leverage the stories of people in your upline or company. I do this all the time.

One of my favorite stories to tell is about my friend Rachel. She is a wife, mother of two, and had a career as a pharmaceutical sales rep. Every day, she had to commute into New York City early in the morning, and because of the nature of her work, she would return home late at night. She missed being home with her babies, so she wanted to find an alternative means of earning an income. She got involved with network marketing and focused on building a business that would liberate her from long commutes and time away from her family. Within twelve months, she was able to quit her job and work her business from home. It totally changed her lifestyle, improved her family dynamics, and today affords her the opportunity to work her business from anywhere. I tell this story to every Mom or Dad who would like to be at home with their children. It creates an emotional feeling and opens the door to talk about the lifestyle enhancement that network marketing can provide.

**Your Personal Story**

It's one thing to tell the story of others, but telling your personal story allows you to develop a special bond with your prospect. You want to craft your story around the products you are offering. Explain why you use the product, how it makes you feel, and the benefits it can provide. Those are all compelling parts of your story. You also want to create a business story worth telling. As I mentioned earlier, keep to the lifestyle benefits of the business model. How the business has improved your lifestyle or the fact that you are building a network marketing business to move toward a better lifestyle is much more relatable than the science or ingredients of a product.

People also relate to financial problems that the business model has solved. In other words, struggling to pay your rent, pay for your child's daycare, or handle all the credit card debt you have accumulated are problems many can relate to. Packaging a story around how you had a problem and how it was solved by building a part-time network marketing business will be very compelling to people you interact with.

In my case, I have been offering health and wellness products for almost twenty years. With every conversation I have, it seems like the same topics come up. We talk about family, friends, business, and how we all are getting older and trying to stay in shape. As you can imagine, these conversations offer a lot of opportunities to talk about the benefits of my wellness products or network marketing business.

I'm always listening for people to speak of a challenge they may be experiencing. Maybe they are unhappy with their current job, looking to get in better shape, lacking energy, or they don't have plans for a summer family vacation. These are just a few of the hundreds of topics people can bring up in conversation that I have a solution for.

When someone talks about getting in better shape, I can tell him my story of feeling great based on the products I consume and then ask him whether he would like to learn more. If he makes a comment about needing to make more money or how he feels frustrated with work, I usually ask him what he knows about network marketing. The answers are always different, but it puts me in the situation to explain what network marketers have been able to accomplish, how we own our lives, and how I may be able to help the person.

The most important aspect of telling your story is to keep it authentic. People know what's real versus what's fabricated. If you have not achieved your financial goals with your network marketing business, let people know that it takes time and that the profession is your vehicle for achieving the lifestyle you are looking for. Don't be that person who fakes it till she makes it. I've always been challenged by those who embellish their stories to sound like they have become millionaires in network marketing just because they have earned a million dollars over their career. Seriously, when you incorporate expenses, taxes, and other living expenses, someone who earns a million dollars over many years is far from being a millionaire.

### Your Team Member's Story

Those of you who are parents know how proud you are when you tell the story of one of your child's accomplishments. It's very gratifying, and you can't tell it enough.

The same applies with telling the story of someone in your organization. Telling this individual's story is more powerful than telling your upline's story. And in some cases, it can be more impactful than telling your own. Reason being, this person joined the business after you, so you played a role in his or her success. This is my favorite story to tell, and I do it every day. By telling a team member's success story, you create a mental picture for your prospect. He hears the story, but he also sees that he will get the same support to help him create a success story of his own.

One of my favorite tools to use when prospecting is a third party tool called *Prosper Magazine*. It's published by Sound Concepts. You can arrange to have your company featured in the magazine; the articles usually focus on the owners, mission, products, and other factors applicable to a business. But the majority of the publication is dedicated to stories of people who have had success with the business and products. What I really love about it is the diversity of the people featured and how so many people can relate to them.

The particular issue I use features people from all walks of life, including business professionals, single moms, entrepreneurs, blue collar employees, and doctors. One of my favorite *Prosper* stories was about my friend Sonia. She is a successful real estate agent who found network marketing by chance. She was just a customer of the products and had never been involved in network marketing before. She had such great results using the products that she felt compelled to share them with others. In just two years, she was able to build a residual income that surpassed the income she was making in her real estate career. What's really cool is that it was her first go at network marketing. Stories like this are not uncommon today since people are now finding this industry for the first time and succeeding faster than they would have in the past.

All three of these story types are powerful and effective. And unlike explaining facts, figures, and ingredients, they are relatable by the people you tell them to. You won't feel like you are selling and the person you're talking to won't feel like he or she is being sold to. The moral of this story is there are people succeeding in this profession from all walks of life. Learn their stories, tell them to those who can relate, and discover how you will harness the power of telling stories.

**Exercise**

Who is someone in your upline you can tell a success story about? What is that story?

_____

_____

_____

_____

_____

_____

What are the key points of your own story that you can tell?

_____

_____

_____

_____

_____

_____

Who is a team member whose story you can tell? What makes that story relatable and exciting?

_____

_____

_____

_____

_____

_____

# Part III

# Building a Team

"Great things in business are never done by one person. They are done by a team of people."

— Steve Jobs

In the previous section, I wrote about taking action with your business. I focused on the importance of launching your business and duplicating it with a system. You learned how to create a daily method of operation focused on income-producing activities and how to become an effective promoter of events. And finally, I spoke to the power of social media and how becoming a compelling storyteller will help you attract people to your business.

If you implement what you learned in the previous section, you will have ripples happening everywhere in your business. As a result, you will start to develop a team of people. There's nothing more exciting than that feeling you get when it's not just you. You have a group of people attending the events with you, and you're starting to experience the leverage aspect of the business model. If you are already there, congratulations! You're getting paid on the efforts of others.

Network marketing is an interesting team-building exercise because everyone who is participating owns his or her own business. In order to succeed, everyone needs to make his own prospecting calls and do his own follow-ups. Where the team building comes into play is in supporting each other through the process and empowering others to succeed.

## CHAPTER 11

# FINDING THE RIGHT PEOPLE

"The strength of the team is each member.
The strength of each member is the team."

— Phil Jackson

Basketball player and coach John Wooden was a well-respected leader. As head coach at UCLA, he won ten NCAA national championships in a twelve-year period, including a record seven years in a row. To this day, no other team has won more than two in a row. During his tenure, Wooden's teams won a men's basketball-record of eighty-eight consecutive games. Wooden was named national coach of the year six times.

Those who know sports or followed Wooden's philosophy know that he was very inspirational to his players. I once watched an interview in which he was asked why he thought he was so successful as a coach and leader. His response was very profound. He said that he attributed a large part of his success to finding and attracting the right people, and then getting the most out of them. He didn't say the best people; he said *the right people*. Identifying talent was important, but finding people with character and good values was more important.

In building your network marketing business, you should think like John Wooden did. Look for people who possess good character and values. Their influence and reputations are driven by what people think of them, but in the end, it's their characters that will drive their actions. I can't overemphasize the importance of good character and integrity. The only asset you have when choosing network marketing as a career is your relationships with other people. These relationships are driven by your personal character and how you communicate with people. If you treat people well, have their best interests in mind, and focus on doing the right thing, great things will happen in your business. But before you can attract people of good character, you need to become a person of good character yourself.

Network marketing is a fascinating business because it consists of all kinds of people with different backgrounds and personalities. What I've noticed over the years is that like attract likes, and the only people who last the test of time are those who have good character. As my friend Harris always says, "Time will either expose you or promote you."

What are other common characteristics you should look for in people? Positive people who have a burning desire for change in their life. People who are motivated, passionate about helping others, and willing to put in the work necessary to grow as a person. It also helps if they are coachable, team players, and have a huge desire to win at the game of life. They should tend to be goal-oriented, have a large center of influence, and be capable of empowering others. These people tend to be community leaders, successful entrepreneurs, and business-minded people who know how to get things done.

My favorite prospects are those I call the "successful discontents." These people have been successful in their careers or businesses, but they are looking for change. They are still motivated, need to continue to earn an income, and are open to a new challenge where they can apply their talents, skill sets, and resources. Think about this for a minute: Whom do you know who fits that description? Now let me ask you a question: Why have you not contacted that person about your business? For most people, the answer is: Fear. Fear of rejection, and fear of what others will think about you and your home-based business.

So what do most people do? They get excited about their opportunity, don't make a written list, and contact the five or ten people on their speed dial. You know, those friends and family members on the "safe list." These are your closest friends and relatives whom you speak to on a regular basis. Chances are they probably won't totally reject you, but if they say yes, it's more likely to appease you. I know this sounds harsh, but it's true. And if you do get rejected by these initial contacts, you tend to take it personally, and then your limiting beliefs keep you from moving forward with your business.

When I first started in network marketing, one of the primary reasons I didn't succeed was because I didn't talk to enough people, and the people I did contact were not the right people. Some were friends who needed a job; others were people who looked up to me so I had influence over them. One of the biggest reasons some people never succeed in network marketing is that they are not able to find, let alone attract, dynamic and motivated people to their businesses. The reasons for this include their lack of credibility, their inexperience, and their fear of reaching out.

If you want to take your business seriously, start with getting organized with your prospect list. The best way I've seen builders get organized is by creating what my friend Shanda calls her "network notebook." It's an ordinary notebook, but it's what you do with it that makes all the difference in the world. Fill it up with the names of every affiliation you've ever had. Go through the exercise of writing down the names of everyone in your cell phone, everyone you truly know who is your Facebook friend, every relative, friend, friend of a friend, etc. Continue by adding anyone you have done business with or know from your church or community. After your first round of names, go back over each name and think about that person's affiliations: Where does he work? Whom does she know? Write those names down as well. Keep in mind that you may not necessarily prospect all these people right away, but it's the exercise of writing the names down that will expand your opportunity to network with an unlimited number of people. Every day you should set a goal of adding one or two people to your notebook.

### Who are the "right people"?

When we make our list, we all have a bunch of average people on it. These tend to be our closest friends, coworkers, and relatives. But for the illustration of finding the "right people," you want to focus on the above-average people you know. Following are the Top 10 Traits I look for when prospecting people for the business:

1. People of influence
2. People who are leaders
3. People who are self-motivated
4. People who are happy and well-liked
5. People of integrity
6. People who have entrepreneurial experience
7. People who get a lot of interaction on social media
8. People who are good communicators
9. People who love to help others
10. People who want more out of life

When you reach out to people on your list, you can use two approaches:

1.  **Direct:** The direct approach is when you speak directly to someone about your product, service, or secondary income opportunity. You need to have a lot of confidence and conviction to do this effectively. Whether you are leading with your product or the business, you want to be clear with your intentions so your prospect can respond accordingly. If you're loose with your approach and wavering between the two, you will come across as not being focused, and more likely than not, be faced with some strong objections. When approaching someone directly, being clear with your intentions and the value you can offer is critical.

2.  **Indirect:** The indirect approach to finding the right people is my favorite. I learned to network through people based on my fear of rejection. I figured if I asked people for their opinions, or focused on getting referrals, I would be less likely to get rejected. I was right, and to this day, it's my go-to prospecting approach.

Let me explain how I use the indirect approach so you can try it for yourself. When I contact someone, especially if I have not spoken to him for a while or he is already successful in business, I start by catching up and having a short conversation. Once the ice has been broken, I say something like this:

"_____, the main reason I'm calling is to get some feedback from you. I've been building a business with a company called _____. Have you heard of it? Well, it's a fast-growing company that formulates, manufactures, and distributes an organic line of nutritional superfoods, and it is looking to expand in the _____ area. I'm helping the company identify people who would like to help it expand and earn a secondary stream of income. I figured you would know some people who might have an interest. If I forwarded you some information to review, would you do me a favor and review it and let me know whom you may know that it may be applicable to? Great, I'll send you a (video, magazine, link to a website, etc.). When can you review it so I can schedule a follow-up?"

I prefer to lead with the business because I believe that no matter what company you represent, "your best product is your opportunity." This approach creates successful conversations 100 percent of the time because I'm not pitching my contact. I'm just telling him what I'm doing, what I'm looking for, and asking who he knows. Over time, you will be surprised by how many people actually have an interest themselves after reviewing the information, assuming the tools you use are compelling and effective.

## Exercise

Take a moment and make a list of the top 10 most successful, influential, and entrepreneurial people you know. These are the right people you want as part of your team. Use the traits and approach outlined above and see what results you get.

1. _____

2. _____

3. _____

4. _____

5. _____

6. _____

7. _____

8. _____

9. _____

10. _____

## CHAPTER 12

# CREATING TEAM CULTURE AND COMMUNITY

*"Coming together is a beginning. Keeping together is progress. Working together is success."*

— Henry Ford

Having the proper culture is important for any organization, but for a network marketing business, it's paramount. Every company I've analyzed has had a unique culture that is usually a byproduct of its ownership and top field leaders. These are the individuals who communicate to the general field, and their personalities, beliefs, and actions dictate the company's culture, and in many respects, the business' longevity.

Some companies put a heavy emphasis on their products and the benefits they provide; others focus on the business opportunity and making money. I believe a happy balance needs to exist between the two. Regardless of what you lead with, the most important factor is that you lead with integrity. Without integrity, you will not attract the type of people necessary to build a sustainable business.

I also believe a company culture needs to operate with a sense of openness and acceptability. A network marketing organization consists of a melting pot of people with all kinds of backgrounds. Having a culture of accepting people regardless of their race, color, experience, or background can be very beneficial to a company. Who is one to judge based on one's experience or lack of? It's the company mission that people are attracted to, so if your company or team culture is accepting and welcoming, you position yourself to build a more powerful organization.

What's important to understand is that culture and community is what's going to keep your organization together. It will play an important role in attracting people to your business, getting them engaged, and, ultimately, keeping them active. Keep in mind that people sometimes join your company or organization just because they want to be involved. I can think of a lot of people I've interacted with in the past who were excited about the results they received with the products and were focused on sharing the story with others, but they also continued to attend events primarily because they loved the people, energy, and personal development they received. At the same time, I can think of a lot of people, including field leaders, who have bounced around from one company to another because they either didn't understand the importance of culture or the people they were following never implemented it.

Building culture and the community that surrounds it is something I'm very passionate about. Whether you are looking to do it for the company at large, or your specific team, here are my top ten ideas—plus a bonus one—that will help you build it strong.

1. **Be mission-driven vs. money-driven:** When you get people to rally around a mission or a cause, amazing things can

happen. Being mission-driven will attract people to your company, enhance your overall message, and significantly increase retention. Missions move mountains. If you focus solely on the income opportunity, people will either make money or they won't. If they don't make the money they are looking for, they will soon defect to the next shiny object.

2. **Create a dynamic recognition program:** People will fall on a sword for recognition. Recognition is not just for rank advancements. Make it a habit always to recognize your team members for every little win they have and show sincere appreciation in the process.

3. **Team calls:** Always have a weekly team call to gather everyone who is actively building a business. On these calls, you can discuss training tips, company updates, team member accomplishments, upcoming events, and so much more. The key is to pass the microphone around. Get people engaged by having different hosts and guest speakers every week. When people feel involved, they build belief, have breakthroughs, take action, and move their businesses forward.

4. **Monthly team training events:** You can only go so far in building your community and culture over the phone or Internet. Get face to face on a regular basis. Meet the people, get to know them, share stories, and learn new skill sets. All of these activities will add value to the culture you are trying to build, enhance relationships, and build glue among your team members.

5. **Book of the month:** As the saying goes, leaders are readers. I've seen some pretty amazing self-development take place when an entire team reads the same book or attends the same industry event. Getting people's mindsets all on the same page can be very powerful.

6. **Attend all major events as a team:** This is a must! Attending events in general, but especially the regionals and annual convention, is a critical part of developing team culture. While at these events, consider hosting team dinners or recap sessions to enhance the experience and build a stronger bond with your team.

7. **Standardize your training:** Having a standardized training is important for building know-how and duplication. It's important for creating the right culture because if it's standardized, you can engage other people in the process, which will help you create that culture of inclusion.

8. **Integrity-based servant leadership:** I probably don't have to elaborate on this point because it is self-evident. No integrity, no business. If you don't want to serve others, no one will follow you.

9. **Do the right thing:** Whether it's life in general or building your network marketing business, you will be faced with having to make constant decisions. Some are harder than others. As I tell my children, "If you do the right thing, you'll never regret it. Don't ever lie because the truth is good enough."

10. **Be happy and have fun:** Most people are building their businesses part-time, and many of them are not operating in fun mode with their full-time jobs. So if you create a fun, loving, and flexible environment with your culture, your team members will want to spend more time building the business. It's all about the Law of Attraction.

**Bonus: Private Facebook Groups:** I discussed creating these groups back in Chapter 9. Social media has created an amazing platform for building culture and community. By creating private Facebook groups of team members or customers, you can enhance relationships, communicate concepts, and build community with a simple post.

**Exercise**

What do you like most about the culture and community of the company you represent?

_____
_____
_____
_____
_____
_____
_____

What can you implement or add to your team or company culture to enhance the experience you and your team members are having?

_____
_____
_____
_____
_____
_____
_____

## CHAPTER 13

# ACTING LOCAL, THINKING GLOBAL

"You don't build a business, you build people.
And then people build the business."

— Zig Ziglar

The network marketing profession has come a long way in the last twenty or so years. When I started my first business back in 1994, all we had was the local weekly business briefing and the Saturday getting started training. There was *no* Internet marketing, *no* Facebook, and *no* Zoom video conferencing. In order to build a long distance business, you had to get in the car, jump on the train, or fly to another state to develop a new market. It was expensive and only a few people were able to do it effectively.

Today, we operate under a completely different paradigm. The Internet, social media, and video conferencing services have created a low-cost, borderless opportunity that is only limited to the countries your company operates in. Today's technology allows you to prospect, enroll, and train your new distributors with ease. Depending on the company you represent, you literally have the ability to build your business on a global basis.

With that said, my advice is to start on a local level when building your business. Once you have created your list of people you want to contact, chances are the majority of them live in the same area as you. There are several key advantages to building on a local level.

- It is easier to get in front of people for launch events and one on ones.
- Getting "belly to belly" and seeing the whites of the eyes helps create accountability and partnership.
- You can build community with your team.
- Team events can be established and have more energy.
- You can be accessible to support your team members.
- A better chance of creating local momentum.

Once you have built a local team, you will find that many people on that team will have contacts and relationships in other states or countries. This will afford you the opportunity to open up new markets and expand your business to other areas, while maintaining and growing your local market.

One of my favorite places to build is in the state of Florida. For some reason, it seems like everyone I come across in Florida is not originally from there. People I've worked with on Florida's east coast tend to have contacts in the Northeast. People I've worked with on the Florida's west coast seem to have a lot of relationships from the Midwest. Regardless of where you are building your business, focus on the opportunity in your backyard first and you'll quickly find yourself branching out.

If you build a strong local business and chase the opportunities as they arise in other markets, you can build a nationwide or even a global business if your company affords you the opportunity to do so.

## CHAPTER 14

# WINNING FRIENDS AND INFLUENCING PEOPLE

"The only way on earth to influence the other fellow is to talk about what he wants and show him how to get it."

— Dale Carnegie

Look at any top income earner in network marketing and you will see a person who understands people. Learning the art of people is really important. This includes learning how to *attract* them, *communicate* with them, build *relationships* with them, and *empower* them.

When people ask me what books they should read to become better businesspeople, one stands at the top of the list: *How to Win Friends and Influence People* by Dale Carnegie. Originally published in 1937, it is still, in my opinion, the only book you need to lead you to success. Carnegie will teach you the fundamental techniques for handling people, six ways to make people like you, how to win people to your way of thinking, and how to be an effective leader. If you have not read it, buy it today! You will immediately become a more effective network marketer.

My favorite section of Carnegie's book is the six ways to make people like you. Succeeding in this business is all about the Law of Attraction. In order to attract people to your product offering, your company, or an opportunity, you first have to attract them to you. And that attraction usually comes down to the relationship you have with them, coupled with the level of trust they have in you. Bottom line: your integrity and how they perceive you make all the difference.

Most of the people I have observed over the years who have not attained their business goals usually lacked credible relationships with others or the skill sets and motivation to go out and build them. In order to do so effectively, you need to attract people to *you* first and foremost. Once people trust you and believe in you, you'll find it much easier to attract them to your business.

Following are the six ways Dale Carnegie suggests you can enhance your ability to attract people to you and my personal thoughts and advice on each.

**1. Become genuinely interested in other people.**
In other words, be interested, not interesting. So often I've watched leaders in network marketing make everything about them: how much money they are making, what kind of car they are driving, and the new house they are living in. These are all just possessions; most people really don't care what you have.

Do you want to attract people to you? Be humble, and focus on being genuinely interested in other people. When you enroll someone new into your business or meet someone new in your organization, ask him or her questions that help you get to know that person. What's his background? What are her dreams? Why is the person in this business and what are his or her ultimate goals? These questions and others will build trust and, ultimately, prepare you to help the person launch his business and guide him through the building process.

## 2. Smile.

A smile is the most powerful magnet on the planet. Think about this today as you scroll through your Facebook feed. What pictures are you attracted to? Yes, the happy people who are having fun and smiling. If you want to attract more people to your business, smile with every step you take. Smile at everyone you come across. Smile when you are talking to team members or prospects on the phone; it will adjust your tone and message, and the person will feel it.

Actions speak louder than words, and a smile says, "I like you. You make me happy. I'm glad to see you." A smile costs nothing, but it provides a huge return. It enriches those who receive, without impoverishing those who give. And it happens in a flash, but the memory of it can last a lifetime. "Nothing left to do but smile, smile, smile!"

## 3. Remember that a person's name is to that person the sweetest and most important sound in any language.

I'm the worst with names, but I can totally relate to this principle. I love the feeling I get when someone calls me by name. I sense that the person is dialed into who I am and sincerely interested in what I have to say. I tend to build trust in the person faster and want to hear more of what he or she has to say. I'm always impressed with people who practice remembering and using people's names. It makes me want to get to know them better.

## 4. Be a good listener.

Encourage others to talk about themselves. People want to express themselves and to be heard. In network marketing, it's important to learn the art of becoming a good conversationalist. We all know those people who love to talk about themselves. Their egos are large, and the only thing that matters is what matters to them. People who talk only about themselves think only about themselves.

So if you want to uncover problems that your products or opportunity may provide the solutions for, become an attentive listener. Ask questions that you feel the person you are talking to would enjoy answering. Encourage him to talk about himself and what his dreams and aspirations are. What does she like most about her career or lifestyle? What would he do if he had more time to focus on his passions? These questions and more will create great conversations and show that you are genuinely interested in who the person is.

Remember, it is human nature for people to be more interested in talking about their problems or needs than listening to others. Therefore, focus on others and you will position yourself to attract them to what you have to offer.

**5. Talk in terms of other people's interests.**
The way to a person's heart is to talk about the things he or she treasures most. In network marketing, this is done best by talking about people's dreams and what drives them emotionally. If you approach people with your network marketing opportunity based on the premise of the money they can make, you will not always engage them. But if you have conversations about their passions, you set yourself up for an opportunity to talk about how the network marketing model can help solve some of their problems or provide the resources and time to do what they love doing more often.

A classic example is a health practitioner I knew who loved helping people improve their health, but she was trapped in a career that focused on sick care. Deep down, she knew that being reactive was not the answer; she wished she had a vehicle where she could be more proactive. I engaged her in conversation to expand not only how she would feel if she could be put in a position to help people with their health, but also to earn a secondary income as a result. As you can imagine, when I introduced her to a product line that could help her and the people she cared about, she was very interested. None of this would have happened if I hadn't spoken to her with her interests in mind.

**6. Make the other person feel important, and do it sincerely.**
One of the big lessons I've learned in building network marketing organizations is people just want to be appreciated. They want to be acknowledged for who they are and what they do. Believe it or not, many people come to network marketing for this alone. They just want to be recognized.

Practicing this principle alone will not only advance your business, but it will increase the residual income you earn. Expressing sincere appreciation to those around you is extraordinarily powerful and gratifying at the same time. Make a practice of sincerely thanking your customer base for supporting your business on a regular basis. When someone on your team has a win, congratulate him or her on the accomplishment; that win could be as simple as breaking through the fear of contacting someone on his "chicken list," conducting his first three-way call, or enrolling his first person. Providing sincere and consistent recognition is one of the most powerful things you can do to enhance your relationships. Do it, and do it often!

Learning how to communicate with people and build relationships is an art of its own, and it will play an integral part in building a successful team.

**Exercise**

On the lines below, write down one situation in which you can apply each of Dale Carnegie's six ways to attract people.

Be generally interested in the other person:

_____

Smile:

_____

Use people's names:

_____

Be a good listener:

_____

Talk in terms of other people's interests:

_____

Make the other person feel important:

_____

CHAPTER 15

# HELPING OTHERS ADVANCE

"Successful people are always looking for opportunities to help
others. Unsuccessful people are always asking,
'What's in it for me?'"

— Brian Tracy

One of the best pieces of advice I received from one of my mentors
was to get out of my own way. What he was basically telling me was
that I made myself the issue while I was trying to build my business.
He suggested that I was more interested in what I was going to make
than in what I needed to do to make it. "This business is not about
*you* and what you can do," he told me. "There is no *I* in team. If you
want to build a successful business, you will need to get your head
around the simple concept of helping others advance."

That was a huge awakening for me. Simply put, he suggested that if
I helped enough people achieve their goals, I would achieve mine.
It took a while to learn the skill sets needed to help others advance,
but once I approached my business with that mindset, things started
to happen.

Today, how much I've helped people is one of the key barometers I use when looking at my business each month. First, I look to see who in the organization advanced during the previous month. I ask myself: Whose volume increased? Whose rank advanced? What pocket of the business has the most new enrollees? The question then becomes: Who am I going to help to advance this month?

Focusing on helping others is a powerful mindset and approach for building your business. If you are constantly working with the newest and most excited people, you will stay on what I call the cutting edge of your business. This approach forces you to focus on helping people advance to the next level they are looking to achieve. It keeps the energy high, and if you're working with the right people, it will lead to a constant stream of new potential business builders.

As with everything else you do, consistency is the key. It's easy to become distracted by your kids' activities, your job, friends who are not building with you, and everyday life occurrences. But if you find a way to stay where the action is happening and you focus on helping others advance, you can always be moving your business forward.

True business builders and leaders tend to take the time with their newly enrolled distributors to help them get started right. As with every successful build, it all starts with the enrollment process and setting the proper expectations. Following are several, but not all, of the things you can do not only to get your new distributors started right, but to help them advance:

- **Conduct a proper business planning session:** This session includes a discussion on why they are building a business, what their goals are, how much time they will commit to building a business, and what the system is they need to follow.

- **Helping with the creation of a contact list:** Too many people skip the most important step of launching a business: the contact list. Helping people create and get organized with their list increases their chance of advancing out of the gate.

- **Being present for the event they host to launch their business:** If you are building with a high-touch approach, such as in-home gatherings, you should be present too.

- **Be available for connect or three-way calls:** Three-way calls are arguably the most effective tool we have in this business. Learning the art of effective three-way calls and conducting them with your team members will advance your business.

- **Help them with the initial training of their new people:** It's not uncommon for the newest person to be enrolled by someone who is brand new himself. Reaching down and helping people get started right will help multiple people advance at once.

- **Recognize them for every accomplishment:** Recognition is one of the main reasons why people are in network marketing. The simplest acknowledgment will empower people to move forward and take it to a new level.

- **"Run through the tape":** Teaching your team members not to let up until the last hour of the month will create more monthly volume and, hence, more rank advancements. It instills a "Never give up" attitude throughout the organization, and it helps people with achieving their goals.

- **Turn them on to personal development:** Team members will hit roadblocks and have self-doubts from time to time.

Guiding people to work on themselves will help them persevere in chasing their goals and dreams.

- **Empower them to take ownership of their businesses:** Helping people advance is one thing. Carrying people across the finish line is another. Help people understand that it is their business, and you are only there to guide and work as a partner.

All of this takes time and sacrifice. To build a successful team in this profession, you first need to get people to know who you are, then get them to like you, and ultimately, trust you. Once the trust is in place, a working relationship can be developed. There's no better way to build that trust than by genuinely lending a helping hand to support others in getting started in or advancing their own businesses.

The other aspect of helping people advance is that it opens your business up to the leverage you need to succeed. As individuals, we only have so much personal influence; once it's exhausted, you have to apply other skill sets to find new prospects to talk to. By focusing on other people as they come into your business, you are constantly increasing the number of people you can teach and mentor.

Being available to support your team members will help them in their businesses and help you in the process. Network marketing is one of the few business models in which you can benefit from teaching people what you know. If you do this in a traditional business setting, you run the risk of the person you teach either taking your job, or becoming a competitor. With network marketing, you can have the best of both worlds.

**Exercise**

List three things you can do to support a team member in his or her business:

1. _____

2. _____

3. _____

## CHAPTER 16

# "TAP-ROOTING" INTO YOUR BUSINESS

*"Alone we can do so little. Together we can do so much."*

— Helen Keller

Do you want to make a lot of money with your network marketing business? If so, you need to learn the art of *tap-rooting*. This skill set is usually reserved for leaders or those looking to emerge as leaders, but it's a really powerful concept worth talking about.

Before I get into it, let me tell you what I've watched a lot of people do when building their businesses. Every time they enroll someone new, they are excited about it; maybe they lead the person to a getting started training, and they become their cheerleader. But then they sit back and wait for that new person to take action and hopefully enroll some new customers or distributors. As new distributors come into the organization, they cheer some more. Maybe they reach down and introduce themselves to the new distributors and give some initial guidance, but then, just as they did with their personally enrolled distributors, they sit back and wait to see what happens. Chances are this semi-passive approach to building a network will not give you the results you are looking for.

Alternatively, you can take a proactive approach to building your business by engaging in the concept of tap-rooting. The best analogy I can offer for this concept is to think about a tree's root system. Every tree has a root system, and it starts with the main root. From that main root there are many offshoots. The offshoots are searching for water and nutrients that will help the tree grow. The same concept applies to building a network of people. You are the tree, and your organization consists of a root system. Just as a healthy tree has an extensive root system, a healthy business will constantly have new distributors entering the organization. Your business needs new distributors just as a tree needs water and nutrients to grow. Tap-rooting will create new activity, help you grow your business, and ultimately, increase your monthly overrides.

The tap-rooting process is top down and starts with those you personally enroll. Let's say you enroll your friend Chet. You want to help Chet, so you help him get started and enroll his friend MaryKay. You then help MaryKay get started, and she enrolls her friend Cindi. Then you work with Cindi to help her enroll her cousin Illana, who enrolls her friend April, who enrolls Marina, who enrolls Rachel.

You keep working through the root system of your network until you find someone who is not only motivated, but has influence, experience, and the leadership skills to build a successful business. When you find that person, you should partner up with him or her and mentor the person to become your next leadership leg. And that, my friends, is the simple concept of tap-rooting to build leaders under leaders.

Obviously, there is more to it and it takes time, but when you build a solid root system within your organization, you build stability, relationships, and layers of leaders. Those leaders tend to take ownership of their businesses and increase your potential for passive residual income.

Of all the industry leaders I've met over the years, the majority of them earn a large portion of their residual income from people they didn't personally enroll, let alone know, before they started their businesses. Most of them achieved this by reaching down and tap-rooting into their organizations, meeting new distributors, and helping them launch their businesses.

Years ago, I started a new organization and did just that. I enrolled a woman named Patty on my first level. Together, we enrolled a mutual friend, and then we continued down that friend's line until we met a couple named Anjila and Geof who happened to be on my fifth level. They were self-starters, had entrepreneurial mindsets, and possessed a lot of influence. We poured all kinds of energy into supporting them to help them succeed and become leaders within the organization. And just as we did to find them, they tap-rooted into their organization and found a person who ultimately became the top income earner in the company. This person was on my thirteenth level and went on to build an organization that produced several hundred million dollars in sales. The benefit of this tap-rooting was huge. Not only did it create a deep-rooted organization of leaders above leaders, but it paid millions of dollars in commissions to the upline, and it continues to pay residual income to this day.

The moral of this story is simple: *You need to be proactive in your business if you want it to grow to its full potential.* Become a talent scout and look for people who have the talents to build it big. One of the amazing aspects of this business is how you can find people more talented than you, help them get started right, and override their success.

Whether you initiate it or not, when you see pockets of activity in your business, don't take them for granted and just become a cheerleader. Reach down and pour gasoline on the fires. Give people recognition for their activity and fast start. Be available to answer any questions or offer advice on how to advance their businesses. This recognition and support will only motivate them to take more action. Keep digging deeper until you find that "diamond in the rough" who takes the lead and ownership of his or her business. It's a lot of work, but it could pay you a residual income for a very long time.

**Exercise**

On a separate sheet of paper, create your tree. Put yourself at the top in the center, then draw roots to your first level people below you. Then draw roots from them to their first level (your second). Do this for your entire network and for as many levels below you as there are. Then circle the people you feel will benefit and can benefit you by your supporting them. Don't forget to update your tree on a regular basis.

## PART IV

# LEADING THE WAY

"If your actions inspire others to dream more, learn more, do more and become more, you are a leader."

— John Quincy Adams

In network marketing, the term "leader" is used a little loosely. I've observed people referring to others as leaders based on their ability to create business volume. I think a leader is much more than that.

I believe that leadership is a privilege. It is a privilege that carries the responsibility to inspire others to achieve their highest and best. I believe that true leaders lead by example. Actions always speak louder than words.

I believe that a true leader within the network marketing profession focuses on creating leaders. After all, there is no success without successors.

Leadership in network marketing, like everything else, will start with you. Do you have the leadership traits that will attract other leaders to you? Are you confident in getting people to follow you?

In this section, we'll look at what truly embodies leadership and the qualities a true leader needs to have to succeed in network marketing.

## CHAPTER 17

# BECOMING THE LEADER YOU WANT TO ATTRACT

"Who you are is who you attract. If you want to attract better people, become the kind of person you desire to attract."

— John C. Maxwell

If you were to ask me, "David, what's the one thing you wish you did earlier in your career as a network marketing professional?" one thing would come to mind. I wish I had studied and learned the art of leadership sooner—and not only how to lead other people, but the characteristics and personal actions required to attract other leaders to my organization. As I write this chapter, I want to acknowledge that I'm probably in the fifth inning of becoming an effective leader. I've had glimmers of leadership light that I've been able to bestow upon some people, but I believe I have a lot left to learn and put into practice.

It's one thing to be a leader to your team. It's another to understand what you need to become to attract other leaders to you. Perhaps you don't feel like you are a leader, and based on your past experiences, you don't believe anyone would follow you. If that's the case, pick yourself up, brush yourself off, and let's focus on what is necessary to become that person you want to attract.

John C. Maxwell is one of the greatest leadership coaches I've ever learned from. His book *The 21 Irrefutable Laws of Leadership* is at the cornerstone of my personal growth library. The ninth law, The Law of Magnetism, gave me an instant aha moment when I read it.

In this law, Maxwell describes leaders as magnets. They are constantly attracting followers, and they often attract new leaders to themselves. This attraction is what causes organizations to experience growth. However, Maxwell cautions that the leadership magnet is one that attracts likeminded people. In other words, the people who wind up surrounding the leader are people similar in nature to him. So if you're negative all the time, the people you attract will be also. And if you're positive, motivated, and productive, you will attract those types of people.

For me, this rule has been an important revelation. You see, I know what sort of people I want to attract into my business and into my life. If I attract those who are like myself, that means it's my job to become the sort of person I would want to attract. When taken into real consideration, this is a truly simple rule to follow, yet its results could be life-changing. Imagine for a moment the ways your life would change as a result of applying this rule and making a tiny change to your attitude or a habit. You could reconstruct your friend circle in a relatively brief time to be more reflective of the type of life you want. The difference maker is you making the decision to do it.

**Exercise**

Let's take a moment and do some self-discovery.

Are you happy with the team around you? Yes/No

Are you pleased with the friends and acquaintances you have? Yes/No

If not, then it may be time for change. Are you willing to become the person you want to have around you? Yes/No

Think about the ideal team you want to build in your business. What characteristics and qualities do you want those team members to have?

_____
_____
_____
_____
_____
_____
_____
_____
_____
_____
_____

Once you've made this list, evaluate yourself.

Are you displaying those qualities? Yes/No

Are you a living example of them? Yes/No

Do you want to be more successful? Yes/No

Work on your personal and professional development. Become the person who attracts top talent and high-quality friends.

Do you want to have a more productive team? <u>Yes/No</u>

Become the person you are wanting to attract so you can attract people of that quality.

In order to have or achieve more in life, you need to become more. Where do you need to start today? Get started!

CHAPTER 18

# SERVING OTHERS LEADS TO A FOLLOWING

"The first and most important choice a leader makes is the choice to serve, without which one's capacity to lead is severely limited."

— Robert Greenleaf

"Why did you join your network marketing company?"

I don't know about you, but when I first got involved with network marketing, I was in it for the money. I saw people as potential customers and distributors who would buy products, build volume, and increase my check. My primary focus was on what I needed to do to maximize the compensation plan. Over time, this self-centered mindset didn't serve anyone but myself. I wasn't malicious or unethical about it; I just didn't know any better. I didn't know how to lead an organization, let alone do it by serving others.

About ten years into my network marketing career, I was introduced to the concept of servant leadership. Up to this point, my leadership skills and philosophy were more centered on telling people what to do versus showing someone how to do it. Again, I just didn't know any better.

While the idea of servant leadership goes back at least two thousand years, the modern servant leadership movement was launched by Robert K. Greenleaf in 1970 with the publication of his classic essay, "The Servant as Leader." In this essay, he coined the words "servant leader" and "servant leadership."

He defined a servant leader as one who focuses primarily on the growth and wellbeing of people and the communities to which they belong. While traditional leadership generally involves the accumulation and exercise of power by one at the top of the organization, servant leadership is different. The servant leader shares power, puts the needs of others first, and helps people develop and perform at their highest levels possible.

So what does servant leadership have to do with network marketing? Everything! It wasn't until I learned the concept of serving others that my business not only flourished, but became more stable. There's a saying I like to use, "There is no success without successors," and the only way to develop successors is to lead others to become leaders themselves. It's been my experience that you can't tell people to lead. First of all, people who join a network marketing business are volunteers. They were not forced to join; they did so because they were looking for change in their lives. So the challenge is to help people see the vision, set their own personal goals, and then trust you enough to follow you. I've watched countless people join network marketing businesses and quit because they were not leaders and didn't have the proper leader to follow. It's a shame, but true.

Servant leadership is all about focusing in on people. Giving without wanting anything in return.

Over the years, I have observed a few true servant leaders in network marketing, and they possessed several key characteristics. But it's the actions they take as a result of those characteristics that make all the difference when building their organizations. Here are the 10 key actions a servant leader must take and key characteristics he must have in order to be successful:

1.  **Be Self-Aware:** Each of us is the instrument through which we lead. If you want to be an effective servant leader, you need to be aware of who you are and how you impact others. People in your organization are watching and reacting to your personality, your strengths and weaknesses, your skills and experiences, the way you talk, the way you dress, and the way you act. You learn a lot about yourself based on others' feedback and how you see yourself. Positive self-awareness and working on yourself will help you as you lead your team.

2.  **Be a Good Listener:** If you want to serve others in life and business, listen to what they have to say. A lot can be learned from other people building out in the field. Be open to others' opinions and feedback. Listen to them when they are having challenges just as much as when they are sharing their triumphs. God gave us two ears and one mouth for a reason; use them.

3.  **Be Empathetic:** Network marketing is a people business, and the best servant leaders I know have the ability to share in what other people are feeling. When people are happy, servant leaders champion their enthusiasm. When they are challenged, servant leaders are understanding and help them through it. Someone once told me, "I dare you to care." Empathy is so powerful, and it puts you in a situation to create a following.

4.  **Help Others:** Successful network marketing leaders know that this is a business of helping others. I don't know of any

other business model where you can spend the time to help others and get paid the way we do. Help your new distributors get started right, be available to do three-way calls with them, spend the time to help them advance to the next rank, teach them a new skill set, and guide them to understand the power of the profession. These are just a few of the countless ways you can help people move their businesses forward by serving their needs.

5. **Coach, not Control:** Coaching and mentoring is a good way to develop people. Network marketing organizations thrive on direction and systems, but trying to control people doesn't bring out their best. Servant leaders bring out the best in their organizations by engaging, inspiring, coaching, and mentoring. Servant leaders help their team members understand the organization's mission and their roles in fulfilling it. Servant leaders make sure their teams understand the organization's goals, and have the training and tools they need to achieve those goals.

6. **Unleash Others' Energy and Intelligence:** After developing and coaching their teams, servant leaders unleash the energy and potential of their up-and-coming leaders. People need experience making their own decisions because occasions may arise when they need to be the leaders or make a decision that they normally don't make. Failing to unleash the energy and intelligence of others is extraordinarily sad and wasteful. It doesn't make any sense to have lots of people in an organization, if only a few—those at the top—use their full potential. Servant leaders unleash others and encourage them to make the maximum contributions they can to the organization and the people it serves.

7. **Be a Steward of Personal Growth:** Everyone is in need of improving his or her wellbeing and personal status in life. Improving self-confidence, developing skill sets, and en-

hancing one's quality of life are all necessary for building a successful network marketing business. Personal development is the answer, and servant leaders not only realize this, but they guide people through the personal development process.

8. **Dream Big:** Great leaders help team members not only to see the potential in themselves, but they encourage them to dream big. I mean really BIG! If you really want to change your life financially, you need to be able to see yourself financially free, living the life of your dreams. Where would you live? What kind of car would you drive? What would your typical day look like? These are only a few of the visions that servant leaders help their team members see.

9. **Build Culture and Community:** The strongest and most stable organizations in this profession were created by leaders who understood the importance of culture and community. Yes, people will enter your program for the products and the opportunity to make some additional money. But they will stay for the culture they resonate with and the community they can become a part of. One of the biggest lessons I've learned as it pertains to building a lasting organization is to serve others by helping them become part of the community.

10. **Sacrifice:** In business, in general, if you want to succeed, you need to make a sacrifice. If you want to be an effective leader within the network marketing profession, putting others first and sacrificing time and activities will only enhance your chance for success.

While there are other practices that help servant leaders to be effective and successful, these are some of the most important. They are about paying attention to people, developing people, and looking ahead so that the servant leader and his colleagues will be able to continue serving others, far into the future.

In the end, you're either leading or following. The followers in this profession are the 80 percent who create the activity to change the lifestyle of the other 20 percent. It's your choice whether you want to lead or follow. Leading doesn't have to be difficult. A simple act of kindness, getting involved with a team call or event, and listening to a team member's needs are all simple acts that can move you in the direction of servant leadership. Serve and others will follow.

**Exercise**

Look at the list of servant leader characteristics above. Rate yourself on a scale of 1-5 with 5 being excellent and 1 nonexistent on how well you are doing at being a servant leader in each category.

Be Self-Aware                                      _____

Be a Good Listener                                 _____

Be Empathetic                                      _____

Help Others                                        _____

Coach, not Control                                 _____

Unleash Others' Energy and Intelligence            _____

Be a Steward of Personal Growth                    _____

Dream Big                                          _____

Build Culture and Community                        _____

Sacrifice                                          _____

Determine which of those characteristics you most need or want to work on and strive to improve at it for the next month. Then the following month, pick another characteristic you can work on, and continue through the process each month with a different characteristic.

## CHAPTER 19

# FACING AND OVERCOMING ADVERSITY

"Every adversity, every failure, every heartache carries
with it the seed of an equal or greater benefit."

— Napoleon Hill

Life is not easy, and neither is building a network marketing business. If it were, everyone would do it.

You will face all kinds of challenges in building your business. Prospects you invite to a presentation will not show up. Your best friend or family member you love will not support you in your new venture. You will set a goal and won't achieve it. Your upline will quit, or worse yet, you won't have the support of your significant other. The person you enrolled whom you are all excited about does nothing. A leader in your business decides to go to another company. You failed to re-qualify at your highest rank. Does this sound familiar? I'm sure you can relate, and if not, get ready because you eventually will. Building a network marketing business, or any other traditional business for that matter, will produce a continuous succession of both small and large problems. No sooner do you get control of one situation than you are hit by another. As network marketers, we are building a business of volunteers—people who have made a personal decision to purchase your product or build a business. I always refer to it as leading or guiding a volunteer army. Because a network marketing organization is a grouping of volunteers, you never know what will arise and how people will react.

So when you face the inevitable challenges and adversity is at your front door, the big question is: How are you going to deal with it? When push comes to shove, when the rubber meets the road, when the chips are down, how you deal with it will define your true character. You learn what you're really made of only when things go wrong and you are tumbled, end over end, by some adversity or setback that hits you like a Mack truck coming out of an alley. Since your behaviors on the outside are the real indicators of who you are on the inside, only by observing how you behave when things go wrong can you tell what you really have inside you.

The starting point in dealing with any difficulty is simply to relax. Clear your mind. Get yourself into a state where you're calm and cool and in full control of your emotions and senses. Back off mentally, and become as objective as possible. Step back and look at the problem with a certain amount of detachment, as if it were happening to someone else. When you can analyze your adversities clearly, you sometimes see opportunities to turn them to your best advantage or come up with the solution that makes it all good.

Over fifty years ago, Dale Carnegie wrote a four-step method for dealing with any adversity. It's still one of the most powerful mental tools anyone can use when confronted with life or business problems, and it's helped me address the adversity I've faced in building my network marketing business.

**Step One: Define the problem clearly.** What exactly is the problem? What exactly are you worrying about? Write out the definition of your problem. Make sure that it's a single problem. If it's more than one problem, write out clear definitions of all the problems that together constitute what you are worrying about right now.

**Step Two: Determine the worst possible outcome.** Ask, "What's the worst possible thing that can happen in this situation?" Be frank and honest with yourself. You might lose your money, or your relationship, or your customer, or someone or something else really important to you. If everything fell apart, what would be the worst thing that could happen?

**Step Three: Resolve to accept the worst, should it occur.** Having identified the worst possible outcome, you now can go through the mental exercise of accepting that it is going to happen, no matter what you do. The remarkable thing is that as soon as you stop resisting the worst possible outcome, you'll relax, your mind will clear, and your ability to deal with the situation will improve dramatically.

**Step Four: Begin immediately to improve upon the worst, which you have already accepted is going to happen.** Throw all of your mental resources into the battle to minimize the problem or resolve the difficulty. Concentrate on the future. Don't worry about what happened, why it happened, or who was responsible. Think only about the question, "What do I do now?" How can you minimize the consequences? What's the first step you can take? And the second step? And the third step? And so on.

Successful people are not people without life problems. They are people who respond quickly and positively to their problems. They think them through in advance; they anticipate them. And when they can't, they use the four-step method to resolve whatever difficulties they face. They define the problem clearly. They define the worst possible thing that could happen as a result of the problem. They resolve to accept the worst, should it occur. And then they concentrate all of their energies on making sure that the very worst doesn't happen.

In dealing with adversity effectively, your ability to ask questions is essential. As long as you are asking questions, you are expanding the range of options and possibilities open to you. As long as you are asking questions, you are keeping your mind calm, cool, and objective. You are not allowing yourself to get caught up emotionally, thereby shutting down large parts of your brain and your creative powers.

Many problems and adversities arise because of misunderstandings and incorrect information. One of the smartest things you'll ever do in facing any adversity is to ask yourself, "Who else may have had this problem, and what did he/she do?" Ask around. Don't be afraid to admit that you're in a bind. If you made a mistake, or dropped the ball and found yourself in a difficult situation, don't be afraid to go to someone and admit that you need help. You'll be amazed by the valuable advice you can get from someone who has already experienced the same difficulty.

In dealing with adversity, perhaps one of the most important positive affirmations you can remember is: "This, too, shall pass." Whatever it is, however difficult it may appear, say to yourself, "This, too, shall pass."

One of your main jobs in building your network marketing business is to become an expert in dealing with adversity. Keep your thoughts on where you're going, not on where you've been. Keep your eyes on your goals and your dreams. Be *grateful* for what you have and where you are. Resolve in advance that you will meet and overcome every difficulty, and then, no matter what happens, don't give up until you do.

**Exercise**

Use Dale Carnegie's four-step method to overcome the current adversity in your life. If you're still trying to decide whether network marketing is right for you, then apply the method to that issue.

What exactly is the problem you are facing? Write a definition of it.

_____
_____
_____
_____

What is the worst possible outcome for this problem?

_____
_____
_____
_____

How will you learn to live with the worst possible outcome if it occurs?

_____
_____
_____
_____

What can you do to improve the situation before the worst possible outcome can happen?

_____
_____
_____
_____

## CHAPTER 20

# HAVING FUN AND
# BEING GRATEFUL

"Be thankful for what you have; you'll end up having
more. If you concentrate on what you don't have,
you will never, ever have enough."

— Oprah Winfrey

Two personal traits can really propel your business even more than
the obvious skill sets and actions: having fun with your business
and being grateful for everything around you. Independent of all
the other principles I've highlighted in this book, if you focus on
these two, you will be successful in life. They can also help you in
becoming a better leader.

**Fun**
You only live once, and you're going to spend a large portion of
your life sleeping and working to make the money needed to support yourself and your family. Typically, you don't have that much
fun while you're sleeping, and the majority of people in this coun-

try wake up on Mondays dreading the fact that they have to go to work. People focus on hump day as the midway point to the week, and they long for Friday so they can have fun on the weekend. If that's what you aspire to, that's cool; just have fun doing it.

If you have fun, you will be more productive and attract more people to your business and way of thinking. People are not looking for another job when they join network marketing. They are looking for a vehicle either to improve their lifestyles, get away from something they are not passionate about, or obtain financial freedom. So if you want to attract people to your business, make it fun.

## Gratitude

Ralph Waldo Emerson once said that in order to achieve contentment, one should "cultivate the habit of being grateful for every good thing that comes to you, and to give thanks continuously."

Turns out Emerson, who explored the meaning of a good life in much of his work, wasn't far off when it comes to what we now know about counting one's blessings. Research is continually finding that expressing gratitude can lead to a healthier, happier, and less-stressed lifestyle.

I believe it can lead to more success in business as well. Life is so fast-paced that it is often difficult to stop to smell the roses and be grateful for what we possess and what we have to offer. I've found that living with a grateful heart takes the stress out of the business-building process and can make you a better leader.

**Exercise**

List five fun things about your business that are fun or list ways you can make it more fun for yourself and everyone involved.

1. _____

2. _____

3. _____

4. _____

5. _____

What are five things you are grateful for?

1. _____

2. _____

3. _____

4. _____

5. _____

# LET THE RIPPLES BEGIN

"Just as ripples spread out when a single pebble is dropped into water, the actions of individuals can have far-reaching effects."

— The Dalai Lama

I hope you enjoyed reading *Ripple Marketing* and gained some real value from my personal experience. Throughout this book, I've shared some of the key principles I've learned on my journey. There is much more to learn, but my hope is that you can apply some, if not all, of these principles to your business and life.

The questions you should be asking yourself are:

What am I going to do with the knowledge and advice I have just received?

How am I going to apply these principles to my business?

Do I now have bigger goals? If so, what are they?

I challenge you to take action and advance your business. Knowledge is not power. "Applied" knowledge is power. You can read all the books you want, and attend all the self-empowerment seminars you can fit into your schedule. But if you don't take action and apply the wisdom you have learned, you won't advance your business or your life.

When you apply your knowledge, you'll be surprised by what will happen. One action—one pebble tossed in still water—can have an incredible ripple effect. Start with that pebble, start locally, but think globally—soon those ripples will spread in ways you could never foresee, and you'll never regret it. Go ahead and throw that pebble.

Here's to your rippling success!

David Skultety

# ADDITIONAL
# RESOURCES

# Selecting the Right Company for You

When I was first introduced to network marketing back in 1994, I honestly didn't know anything about the profession or the companies that were available for me to represent. Not knowing anything about the industry, I actually thought the company I had joined had this unique business model that no other company had. As a result, I thought I had tripped upon the greatest money-making concept known to man.

Like many people who get approached about network marketing, I wasn't looking for an opportunity; it found me. When the company was introduced to me, it was before the Internet became widely available, so there really wasn't a reliable way to conduct due diligence on the company. I had to rely on the person who presented the business and the brochure that was provided. In hindsight, I went on blind faith.

In my case, the first company I joined was a fairly new company that had all the right components. That I didn't succeed with the business is a whole other story. But for many, their first company was not the right company for one reason or another, and when they didn't succeed, they never moved forward to find a company that would work for them. And that is a shame because in many cases, the company failed them.

When you are approached today, you have the luxury of doing your research online and making an educated decision. Furthermore, more and more people are learning about the power of network marketing and are seeking out a company to represent on their own. Selecting the right company doesn't guarantee success, but it does increase your odds. Ultimately, your success in network marketing is determined by what you do. So how do you choose the right company? There are five key factors to evaluate:

1. Owners/Management
2. Products
3. Culture
4. Compensation Plan
5. Start-Up vs. Established

I'll discuss each one briefly.

**1. Owners/Management**
When evaluating a company to represent, you should always start at the top. Who are the owners? What is their experience? Are they properly capitalized? Do they have integrity? Why are they in business? What is their mission? These are just a few of the questions that should be asked. During my travels evaluating companies, I've come across a bunch of them that looked good on the surface. They had well-branded products, an attractive website, and compelling marketing tools. But after looking a little closer at the owners, it was not too hard to see that they'd had some business challenges in the past, had integrity issues, were not mission-driven, or were just in it for the money. If these and similar red flags appear, think twice about representing the company.

Experienced management is also an important factor to consider when evaluating a company. I represented a company that had a mission-driven owner, breakthrough products, and incredible financial resources. But the management hired to run the company didn't have the skill sets or industry knowledge required to grow it to its full potential. This left a wake of well-intended, talented people who didn't achieve their goals because the proper marketing strategy was never implemented.

## 2. Products

Residual income is one of the major benefits and reasons why you should be interested in building a network marketing business. In order to have a chance at residual income, you need to have the right products. When evaluating a company, make sure the products it offers provide value, are not overpriced, and offer a money-back guarantee.

Are the products consumable? Since the business is about long-lasting residual income, the products have to be consumable and of high quality. This leads to repeat purchases by customers, month after month, and year after year.

It's advantageous if the products are unique, patented, and exclusive to the company. Many of the products out there in the profession are private labeled and offered in other places under a different brand. You should only represent products that are unique to the marketplace and in demand.

Consumers *must* also have a compelling reason to buy from your network marketing company, not just to participate in the compensation plan. For example, ask yourself, "Would I purchase these products if I wasn't being compensated to do so?" If the answer is "No," move on to evaluating a different company. Needless to say, you have to use the products. These should be products you are not only comfortable with, but that you feel compelled to share with close friends, family, and anyone you meet.

## 3. Culture

Company culture is more important than ever. It's not that company culture was ever unimportant, but it's quickly proving to be a "must have" rather than a "nice to have." In network marketing, it is no different. A company's culture defines the way people within the organization interact with one another, from corporate to the field, and how the field leaders work together.

Without the proper culture, things can become pretty dysfunctional. Culture is the formula that guides the company's direction and the teams of leaders building the business in the field. It is also responsible for attracting and retaining great field leaders, as well as creating a fun, happy, and exciting entrepreneurial environment.

I've always found it fascinating to go to different company events and feel the difference in energy from one company to the next. Some were dominated by women and some by men. Some were very product-oriented, while others focused on making money. Some companies are catering to millennials, while others seem to attract baby boomers. It is important to identify the culture in the company you want to represent and make sure it resonates with you.

## 4. Compensation Plan

When evaluating a company, you should get a feel for its compensation plan and what you need to do to get paid. Multiple kinds of compensation plans exist today, including the uni-level, binary, matrix, and breakaway. What you ultimately need to know is they all create a specific behavior. Some pay more upfront on product sales, while others move more of the payout to the leaders who build larger organizations. I'm not going to break down the ins and outs of the individual plans, but I want to stress the importance of getting to know the plan and what you have to do to get paid. Optimally, the company you represent should have a plan that is balanced so that the entry level distributors get paid well for acquiring customers, and the leaders who build large organizations can get compensated for their leadership efforts.

### 5. Start-Up vs. Established

Should you join a new start-up company, or an established billion-dollar giant? The most common mistake I see with people joining companies is that they think they need to "get in early" with a network marketing company to make any money. I need to take a moment and debunk that myth. New start-ups can be very exciting, but with them comes a lot of risk. Yes, there is potential high return if they succeed, but the reality is that most do not. I can't tell you how many friends I've watched over the years chase the "shiny new companies," only to be looking for a new company a year or two down the road. Not only does this situation cause financial distress, but it also reduces your credibility among friends and business associates when you keep changing companies and the products you offer.

I'm not going to hang myself by suggesting that there are no solid start-ups worth joining, but I am going to recommend that the average person out there looking to join a network marketing company should consider one that is established and has been in operation for at least five years. A little longevity increases the probability that the company is profitable, well run, and positioned to last the test of time.

Selecting the right company is probably the most important decision you can make when looking to start a career in network marketing. That's not to say that you won't come across problems or challenges with your company. When asked, I often tell people all companies have challenges from time to time. So pick a company and roll with it. Get focused and stay loyal.

# AVOIDING THE 10 DEADLY SINS OF NETWORK MARKETING

Throughout my career, I've watched people self-sabotage their businesses by taking wrong actions in the field while building. Many of their actions could have been avoided by using a little common sense or keeping their integrity in check.

Several years ago, I attended a six-figure summit event sponsored by Eric Worre. It was a great event where Eric and other six- and seven-figure earners shared their best practices with the attendees. During one of Eric's segments, he spoke about the 10 Deadly Sins that every network marketing distributor should avoid. In the spirit of keeping it real, I would like to share that list with you, along with my own thoughts on each sin:

1.  **Over-inflating your product or service:** It is not necessary to embellish the benefits of your product or service. Telling people you have the best products, or the most recent science, or cheapest utility service is not necessary, even if it is true. The truth is good enough, and if your product is that good, it will stand on its own without you telling a fairy tale.

2.  **Lying about your income:** Again, the truth is good enough. There is no faster way to discredit yourself than by telling a lie about the amount of money you or anyone in your company is making. Stretching the truth about your income not only tarnishes your credibility, but puts your company at risk for making income claims.

3.  **Negative talk:** There's a saying in this business that negatives go up, and positives go down. I don't believe in that. I don't feel there is any room for negative talk at all. It's bad

energy, and those who talk negatively are self-sabotaging their businesses. They will bring others down. There is no room for negative talk in building a successful business.

4.  **Inconsistency:** I alluded to this earlier in the book. Being consistent with your daily method of operation with a focus on income-producing activities is one of the keys to success. Those who are inconsistent with building their businesses are not committed to achieving their goals and are setting themselves up for failure.

5.  **Spending more than you make:** This is a big problem with our society in general, and it happens all the time with people in network marketing. I constantly see people flashing fancy cars, shiny watches, and houses they cannot afford. In many cases, these items are purchased before the taxes are paid, and that leads to all kinds of problems. My financial advice is simple: Earn as much as you can, spend the least amount possible, and pay yourself first via a tax-deferred retirement plan. It's not what you make; it's what you keep.

6.  **Stealing prospects or distributors:** How would you feel if you sent a prospect to a meeting in another city, and someone at that meeting told your prospect that he would be better off working with his local group? Exactly. Not good and you would lose trust in the system. Always support guests when they attend your meetings. Also, do not suggest to a cross line distributor that she would be better off on your team vs. the team she is enrolled in. It's dishonest, and karma will come back to bite you.

7.  **Sleeping around in the group:** Yes, I said it, and I've watched it happen. It can destroy not only your integrity, but another person's family. There is no better way to lose the respect of others than to cross this line.

8.  **Public drunkenness:** Network marketing events are a lot

of fun, and many people visit the bar after the day's activities. I'm not saying it's bad if you drink alcohol. I'm just saying that if you drink too much, you could diminish how people see you.

9. **Hogging the spotlight:** Nobody likes an egotistical distributor who makes himself the issue. Such people talk too long when given the microphone. They take too much credit for the business they override. And they don't recognize the people who took them to the top. Don't be this person!

10. **Success Coma:** When you become successful in your business, don't sit back and become a manager of your organization. You are entitled to take some time for yourself since this is the ultimate lifestyle business. But don't take your success for granted. Always be moving your business forward and helping others grow.

# INDUSTRY STATISTICS

As reported on June 2, 2016 by the
World Federation of Direct Selling Association.

## SALES TREND (ANNUAL SALES IN $)

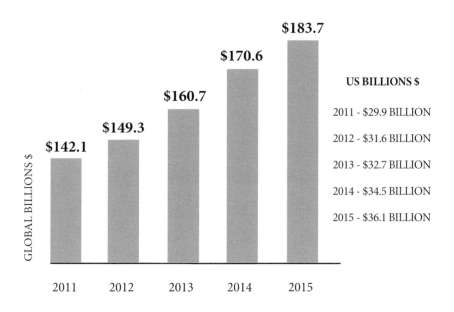

**US BILLIONS $**

2011 - $29.9 BILLION

2012 - $31.6 BILLION

2013 - $32.7 BILLION

2014 - $34.5 BILLION

2015 - $36.1 BILLION

## SALESFORCE SIZE TREND
## (# OF DIRECT SELLERS)

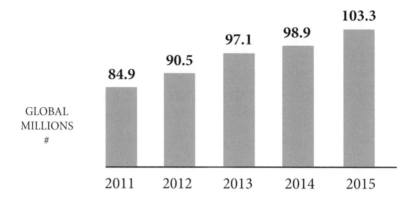

## TOP TEN GLOBAL MARKETS - 2015

| | |
|---|---|
| UNITED STATES | $36.1 BILLION |
| CHINA | $35.5 BILLION |
| KOREA | $16.9 BILLION |
| GERMANY | $15.2 BILLION |
| JAPAN | $14.7 BILLION |
| BRAZIL | $9.1 BILLION |
| MEXICO | $6.9 BILLION |
| FRANCE | $4.6 BILLION |
| MALAYSIA | $4.4 BILLION |
| UNITED KINGDOM | $4 BILLION |
| OTHER | $36.3 BILLION |

**TOTAL $183.7 BILLION**

## GLOBAL SALES BY PRODUCT CATEGORY - 2015

| | |
|---|---|
| CLOTHING & ACCESSORIES | 6.6% |
| COSMETICS & PERSONAL CARE | 31.5% |
| HOME CARE | 2% |
| HOUSEHOLD GOODS & DURABLES | 11.4% |
| WELLNESS | 33.6% |
| BOOKS, TOYS, STATIONARY | 1.9% |
| FOODSTUFF & BEVERAGES | 1.6% |
| HOME IMPROVEMENT | 2.5% |
| UTILITIES | 2.9% |
| FINANCIAL SERVICES | 3% |
| OTHER | 3% |

# ABOUT THE AUTHOR

David Skultety has been in the network marketing profession for over twenty years. Through the companies he has represented, he has mentored thousands of people to take control of their financial futures and guided them to become lifestyle entrepreneurs.

For the first four years of his career, David failed miserably. In 1999, he became a distributor for a health and wellness company and built an organization of over 300,000 people who produced over $500,000,000 in wholesale sales. He then accomplished what very few have done. He started a new business from scratch and built an entirely new organization from 1-100,000 people all over again.

Many who know David consider him a "networker's networker." His reputation for keeping it real and genuinely serving others has earned him the respect of many throughout the profession.

Outside of business, David is a devoted husband and grateful dad to three amazing teenagers. He enjoys playing golf, going to concerts, traveling, and chilling out with friends. His life philosophy is centered on the 5 Fs: Faith, Family, Friends, Freedom, and Fun.

To learn more about David or to contact him directly, visit his website at:

**www.DavidSkultety.com**

# LEARN NETWORK MARKETING FROM DAVID SKULTETY PERSONALLY

Do you want to learn even more about network marketing?

Do you want to have David Skultety personally guide you?

David is available for:

Consulting

Coaching & Mentoring

Lifestyle Retreats

To learn more about David Skultety and the entrepreneurial services and resources he offers, visit him at:

**www.DavidSkultety.com**